frog or prince?

 www.trafford.com

North America & international
toll-free: 1 888 232 4444 (USA & Canada)
phone: 250 383 6864 ♦ fax: 250 383 6804 ♦ email: info@trafford.com

The United Kingdom & Europe
phone: +44 (0)1865 487 395 ♦ local rate: 0845 230 9601
facsimile: +44 (0)1865 481 507 ♦ email: info.uk@trafford.com

10 9 8 7 6 5 4 3 2

frog or prince?

The SMART GIRL'S GUIDE to BOYFRIENDS

KAYCEE JANE

To my daughter: this is my love letter from me to you.

table of contents

introduction

 $\mathcal{E}ver$ wonder why it's so hard to figure out if your boyfriend is the right guy for you? After all, he tells you he loves you, lends you his favorite T-shirt, kisses you like no other guy ever has. Nobody else has made you feel so alive and happy. You can't believe how lucky you are! But he also calls you names, breaks his promises, treats you like a beer slave at parties, accuses you of wanting to sleep with his best friend. So is this guy a Frog or a Prince? A little of both? Confused? You're not alone.

As women, we're hard-wired to seek love. We're on a quest to love and be loved. We grow up believing that when we do find the guy who loves us, we'll be happy forever. Remember the daisy game? You pull off the first petal: "He loves me." And then the next: "He loves me not." We hope the last petal is "He loves me."

In the real world, the daisy game gets us nowhere. Yet if you turn the game around —"I love him, I love him not"— a new question arises: "Is he the right guy for me?" And this leads to an answer that will get you somewhere. How? By making you look at your own needs first.

natalie's story

Natalie believes that if she follows her heart, she'll get to live happily ever after. For the past year, she's felt that her life has become ho-hum. Her family is boring, college classes are boring, hanging out with friends is boring. She envies Meghan, her best friend, who's been going out with Ben for six months and who seems to be so *alive*, "growing happy" all the time. Natalie finds herself daydreaming about a handsome Prince, a guy who'll come along in his elegant carriage (actually a red, late-model BMW) and change her life into the fairy tale Meghan seems to be enjoying.

One day Natalie's in the student cafeteria listening to her iPod. (She's skipped philosophy class again.) Her eyes are closed and she's really into the music, so when someone taps her on the shoulder, she's startled and a little annoyed. But when she gets a look at the culprit — a guy asking if he can sit at her table — she's temporarily speechless. The guy is drop-dead hot, with a smile and a voice that send shivers up her spine. When she comes to her senses and invites him to sit, they immediately get into a great conversation.

His name is Ethan. She finds him warm and attentive, and she keeps looking into those deep-blue eyes, lovely pools she could fall right into. When Ethan smiles at her, she knows what it means to feel alive and grow happy. Before he heads off to class, they exchange contact info. As soon as he leaves, she calls Meghan.

Before long Natalie and Ethan are seeing each other (creating a new outfit crisis every date, which she solves by blending the contents of her closet and Meghan's). She knows that Ethan is attracted to her by the way he noticed her right off the bat. She knows he desires her because he can't keep his hands off her when they're alone. She knows he likes her as a person, too, because he wants to spend all his time with her.

(In fact, his friends — and hers, for that matter — are starting to feel abandoned and a little pissed off.) All Natalie knows is that when she looks at Ethan or spends time alone with him, she has intense feelings of love. She's never felt this alive before — everything is easier to do, and she has bundles of energy. She gets up early and rushes over to borrow Meghan's blue sweater before she studies for her criminology test, then meets Ethan for a fast-food lunch.

A few months later, the blissful feeling wears off a little. The force driving Natalie to meet Ethan's needs starts to feel like work. One Saturday, while they're watching TV, he suggests they go out.

NATALIE: Sure.
ETHAN: What do you feel like doing?
NATALIE: I don't know. What about you?
ETHAN: I asked first.
NATALIE: I don't care, baby. Anything.
ETHAN: Do you want to go out or not? Maybe we shouldn't...
NATALIE: Huh?

At this point, expectations, reasonable or unreasonable, don't get met and their squabbles — fights about nothing — begin.

ETHAN: Hey you, go get me a glass of water. (Gives her a big kiss)
NATALIE: Go get your own.
ETHAN: I got you one last time you asked.
NATALIE: I don't feel like getting up.
ETHAN: Sure about that? (Tickles her until she gets him his glass of water. A few minutes later he asks her to make him a sandwich)

NATALIE: Ethan, I'm into this show. Go make your own.

ETHAN: You make it...

NATALIE: Stop it. I'm missing a good part...

ETHAN: What's more important to you — the show or me? (He goes on and on until she gets up, turns off the TV and gets into a yelling squabble with him)

Natalie finds herself doing girlfriend duties she doesn't really want to do.

ETHAN: Hey, Nat, the guys are coming over tonight and we're gonna watch some DVDs. Can you run over to Flick Picks for us?

NATALIE: No, Ethan, I'm not doing that. I have to pick up Meghan or we'll be late for the movie.

ETHAN: Come on, she'll understand. All you'll miss is the trailers. Please, baby.

NATALIE: Okay, fine, Ethan, what movies do you want?

Fast-forward to the middle of the relationship. There have been lots of changes. The biggest is that Ethan has gone back to his old life and routines — the ones that pre-dated Natalie — while she hasn't gone back at all. She's still eager to spend as much time with him as she can. She's confused, so when she sees Ethan's best friend in the library, she approaches him.

NATALIE: Hey, Tim. Can I talk to you?

TIM: Sure, what's up?

NATALIE: Anything going on I should know about?

TIM: What do you mean?

NATALIE: Well, Ethan hasn't been himself lately. He seems really distracted. Has he said anything about me?

TIM: He hasn't mentioned you in a while, Nat, and he seems the same as always.
NATALIE: Okay, then. Just checking. Thanks for the chat.

The next day she meets Ethan.

ETHAN: What are you doing flirting with my friends?
NATALIE: What?
ETHAN: Why were you talking to Tim?
NATALIE: I'm just trying to understand you. You never tell me what's going on.
ETHAN: Come on, you were flirting with him.
NATALIE: Look, Ethan, I have a rule about flirting. I never flirt with my boyfriend's friends, never mind his best friend.
ETHAN: Whatever. So, do you think he's cute?
NATALIE: Ethan —
ETHAN: You wanna sleep with him, is that it?

He storms out, slamming the door. Natalie immediately calls Meghan.

MEGHAN: Don't worry, Nat. He just doesn't know you well enough yet to know you'd never flirt with Tim.
NATALIE: You think so?
MEGHAN: We have rules about flirting. Didn't you tell him?
NATALIE: Yeah, but it didn't seem to matter much.
MEGHAN: Sounds like Ethan's one of those guys who doesn't tell you when his feelings get hurt, but you know because he gets angry. Besides, he's jealous because he's crazy about you. Don't worry. He'll call you later.

Natalie hangs up feeling better but unsure what will happen next. She leaves Ethan a message, and when she gets home she puts on Ethan's old T-shirt, then sends him an email, explaining why she did what she did. The next morning he hasn't called her back yet, so she cuts class to meet Meghan (wondering what she'd ever do without her). After they chat, Natalie feels strong. On the way to her next class, she uses her sexy-kitty voice to leave Ethan another message. He calls her back and they go through the enjoyable make-up part of their relationship.

More changes take place in the relationship. Ethan's opening lines in many conversations shift from "Hey baby, I'm on my way" to "I don't really feel like going to your parents' tonight." He spends more time with Tim, and Tim treats Natalie differently, becoming distant. None of this makes sense because she's worked hard to please Ethan; to have a great relationship, she believes, you have to please your boyfriend. Ethan has also become critical of her; his new favorite line begins "I'm not happy that you…" She can't understand because she jumps through hoops to meet his needs. She's trying to give him what he asks for and to let him get his way without being a total doormat. In return, it seems, he's become less attentive, often not even returning her calls or ignoring her when they're out with his friends. It seems he's bored with her.

Meghan suggests she try to spice up the relationship by making plans that she knows interest him.

NATALIE: Hey, let's go to Playland this weekend. You haven't been on that old roller coaster since you were a kid. And you really used to love it, didn't you?
ETHAN: I can't believe you remember that.
NATALIE: Great! Should I ask Meghan and Ben too?
ETHAN: I can only go if Tim doesn't need help with his car.
NATALIE: When will you know?

ETHAN: I'm not sure. I'll let you know.
NATALIE: (disappointed) Okay then.
ETHAN: Hey, get over here. (Leans in to give her a kiss)

She doesn't get why Ethan doesn't want to do stuff with her as much as he did before, but she hopes it'll blow over and they'll get back to the way it was in the beginning. Then it seems her wish comes true: they have a "Let's put our relationship back on track" night and have so much fun she can't even find the words to describe it to Meghan.

But this lovely interlude doesn't end their squabbles. One of their rerun arguments is about who gets to pick what to do: what TV show to watch, what station should be on the car radio. Ethan's stubborn about getting his way and phrases like "Good point, Nat. Sure, it's your turn" just don't come up. Natalie is baffled by why they fight over these things. She finds herself giving in just to keep him happy.

Lately, things have been getting really confusing. Stuff comes up that has nothing to do with what she and Ethan started fighting about. This stuff is actually a list of what Natalie hasn't been doing for him lately; the things she *does* do for him are never mentioned. Sometimes she just stares at him. She can't believe what she's hearing. What he's saying is not true, but she doesn't know exactly why. She worries that he's growing to know her by what she doesn't do for him, but then she throws her own list of his "won't do's" at him, too. The last time they had one of these ugly arguments, Natalie felt so messed up she had to back out of her promise to help with a birthday dinner for Meghan's dad, which was *so* not her! But Natalie felt that if she hadn't stayed to fix things up with Ethan, they wouldn't still be together.

When Natalie thinks about how stuff with Ethan is affecting her friendship with Meghan, she feels a little anxious. She hasn't been as good a friend to Meghan since she started seeing

Ethan; in fact, the time they do spend together gets eaten up with "Ethan this" or "Ethan that," so actually she's lost track of what's going on in Meghan's life.

Lately, Ethan has started disappearing with Tim for long stretches without telling Natalie what he's doing; it's starting to feel like Tim has stolen her special spot in Ethan's life. Last night, for instance, he called her to cancel their plans. Of course, he couldn't tell her the reason, mumbling instead, "This just came up. I'll talk to you tomorrow. Gotta go." Next morning she learned what "this" was when Sara, a girl they all hang out with, called and asked why she hadn't shown up at Michael's with Ethan.

> SARA: By the way, Nat, have you met Gwen's new friend, Ella?
> NATALIE: Yeah, I met her at that beach party last weekend with everybody else. She seemed really nice.
> SARA: She was at the party last night, too. I was surprised you and Meghan didn't show up. Elizabeth was there…

The call ends with an awkward goodbye. Natalie wonders if Sara was trying to tell her something or just stirring up trouble. She immediately tries Ethan on his cell; she leaves a message.

Then Meghan calls her, upset about *her* life. Natalie heads over to talk, but not before telling her what Sara just revealed about Ethan. Then, just as she's pulling into Meghan's driveway, her cellphone rings. It's Ethan, who has obviously picked up her message: "Hey baby, get your butt over here. I love you. We need to talk." Natalie says a too-eager yes because anything Ethan says right now will make her feel better. Meanwhile, Meghan watches Natalie pull into and then back out of her driveway. Natalie calls her.

NATALIE: Look, I'm sorry. I just got a call from Ethan. Do you mind if we talk later?

MEGHAN: Natalie, Ethan lied to you last night so you wouldn't show up at Michael's. When are you going to get it?

NATALIE: Maybe he just needed some space. Besides, he just told me he loves me and wants to talk this out.

MEGHAN: You're so different since you've been going out with this guy.

NATALIE: I am not! I love him. I can't imagine my life without him.

MEGHAN: Come on, Nat. You need to break up with him. Anyway, call me after you're done with Ethan.

NATALIE: I will. Sorry. You do understand, right?

Natalie calls her back next morning to tell her everything's good again with Ethan and she's on her way to pick her up for coffee. Later on, Natalie runs into Elizabeth, who she was going to call to get "Ethan information." Since Elizabeth doesn't have any juicy Ethan bits from Michael's party, the conversation moves to Natalie's love story. Before Elizabeth runs off to music rehearsal, she promises to think about what Nat confided and call her later. Natalie looks forward to talking things through with Elizabeth to make more sense of her Ethan feelings. The next morning all hell breaks loose when Ethan calls Natalie, fuming.

ETHAN: Natalie, what were you thinking gossiping to Elizabeth about us?

NATALIE: What?

ETHAN: You know she's crushing on Tim. Did you think I wouldn't find out?

NATALIE: I wasn't gossiping —

ETHAN: You expect me to believe that?

NATALIE: Yes, Ethan. I do. You're acting like I betrayed you and —
ETHAN: Come on, you were talking behind my back!
NATALIE: I wasn't! I'm confused about some stuff....
ETHAN: Sure, whatever.
NATALIE: Ethan...I love you. Maybe talking to Elizabeth was a bad idea.
ETHAN: You think? (Ethan hangs up)

Natalie calls Meghan to tell her what just happened.

MEGHAN: I can't believe Elizabeth would do that.
NATALIE: Yeah, well — she did.
MEGHAN: She was probably trying to get info from Tim about Ethan — to tell you.
NATALIE: I don't know what to think.
MEGHAN: Call her and find out.
NATALIE: Meg, I can't. What if Ethan hears about it?
MEGHAN: You and Elizabeth are friends. You have to work this out.
NATALIE: I don't know what to say to her.
MEGHAN: What?
NATALIE: I don't want to fight with Elizabeth about this too. It's just too hard right now.

As usual, she and Ethan muddle through the drama and move to the make-up part. She holds on tight to the hope of love as her happy experiences grow further apart. She doesn't have a clue about what's going on, and she finds herself unsure and struggling to figure it out. The joy she once felt when she thought about Ethan is being replaced with an anxious feeling in the pit of her stomach.

Still, she's looking forward to the camping trip on the long weekend. She drifts off dreaming of putting up the tent with

Ethan and building a little nest, canoeing, swimming, cuddling by the fire...

The next day he calls and says he'll pick her up at seven — he's taking her to dinner. The evening starts well, but the conversation takes an unexpected turn.

ETHAN: I need to talk about something important.

NATALIE: Okay...

ETHAN: Well...

NATALIE: Hey, remember we have to sort out our plans for the camping trip.

ETHAN: Yeah, well, here's the thing. Listen, I really love you and you're great....

NATALIE: Ethan, what are you trying to say?

ETHAN: I think we should break up.

NATALIE: What? When did you figure this out? I mean, you just said you loved me!

ETHAN: It's more like a break, not a break-up. I need a time-out to figure out some stuff. I love you, Nat.

NATALIE: So we're not breaking up — we're just on a break? What does that mean? Can we see other people?

ETHAN: Nat, that's not what this is about. It's about me.

NATALIE: What are you talking about? Of course this includes me! What about the camping trip — are we still going together?

ETHAN: I don't know — I don't think so.

Ethan doesn't seem to have more answers. Later, when they pull up in front of her house, she puts her arms around his neck. It feels so sweet and good she wishes he'd tell her he's changed his mind. She gets out, biting back tears. Before he pulls away, he rolls down the window and tells her he loves her and he'll call tomorrow.

By the weekend Meghan has convinced Natalie to go camping anyway, saying she can hang out with her and Ben and the rest of the group. Besides having fun, she'll have a chance to spend time with Ethan. Unfortunately, it doesn't work out that way. She spends the weekend watching Ella and Ethan's budding love unfold, all the while listening to Ethan deny that anything is going on. Mostly she wishes she were anywhere but on this stupid camping trip, except for during and right after her talks with Ethan. But those talks do not get her any closer to the make-up part, and she can't help thinking that Ella is so much prettier and thinner than she is.

A couple of weeks later, Meghan tells her that Ethan and Ella are officially going out. The parties go on, but now Ethan and Ella show up together, with Tim in tow, and Natalie shows up unattached. Feeling like an outcast in her own circle is just too hard, so to fix the hurt she starts to build Ella a nasty reputation. As for Ethan, at first she hates him, but then she decides to keep him "on reserve." Who knows, he and Ella might not last...

what went wrong?

Going out with a guy is about choosing to share yourself with another person who is special to you in a different way from anyone else. You always hope the guy is going to be your Prince, but life doesn't usually work out this way. Princes and Frogs can be hard to tell apart: Princes are not perfect and Frogs are not necessarily bad guys. So making a good boyfriend choice — choosing a Prince rather than a Frog — is tough.

Once we're in a relationship it can get even tougher, especially when we believe we should follow our heart. Even when our friends and family tell us that the guy we're with isn't the right guy for us, we tell them (and ourselves) over and over that everything will be okay. After all, our guy keeps promising he won't do this or that anymore (whatever this or that may be), and we believe him. We love him. We can't imagine our life without him. We have so much invested in the relationship it's too hard to think about not being able to work things out with him — to accept that he might not love us enough. So we tell ourselves that yes, love hurts (as the songs say), and we should accept our guy, Frog warts and all. These beliefs can lead us, like Natalie, to decision disasters, where we try with all our might to build a healthy relationship with a Frog, which — by the way — is impossible.

Natalie's a smart, strong, beautiful young woman who plans to become a lawyer. So how did she get herself into such a painful relationship with a Frog like Ethan? The answer is that while she has a lot going for her, she isn't equipped with enough self-knowledge, information and tools to choose a Prince — let alone build a relationship with one. She mistakenly believes that when you add a boyfriend to your life, you automatically start growing happy. Life doesn't work that way. There are no Princes in shining carriages who come along and hand us a beautiful life.

When Natalie met Ethan she didn't know what needs she deserved to get fulfilled in the relationship. Sure, she felt as if all her needs were met at the beginning — and then some — but she didn't have a concrete idea of what needs she deserved to get met. We don't just wake up one morning knowing what needs we deserve to have fulfilled in a relationship. Wouldn't life be great if we did!

Natalie also didn't know what warts she could accept while still maintaining her self-respect. She allowed Ethan — and ultimately herself — to use disrespectful tactics. Because she couldn't see the point at which his Frog warts became too much, she accepted many more life-with-Frog experiences than she should have. Ethan's warts and disrespectful behavior hurt her in a way that made it hard for her to respect herself, or him. She didn't know that who Ethan is as a person — Frog warts and all — determined how well he could meet her needs.

It's hard to see the big picture when making choices, to see what all of your experiences add up to. Even listing positive experiences on the left side of the page and negatives on the right wouldn't give you a clear answer that you could act on. Since Natalie didn't even have a clear picture of what Frog warts were, how many of them do you think she'd have listed? Not a lot, probably. Ethan's good points, on the other hand, would have been plentiful.

Then there's coping amnesia, which is a condition caught from Frogs, usually by kissing and/or listening to Frog-speak (bullshit). This condition erases Frog behavior from a girl's memory, and there is no hard-and-fast rule for how long the condition lasts. For example, Natalie displayed coping amnesia when she forgot how Ethan had treated her, accusing her of wanting to sleep with Tim or using nasty words and names to get his way. Natalie could only (or only wanted to) see the little picture of her relationship with Ethan. Her positive experiences — the affection she got; the "Let's get back on track" night; and his make-up tactics, showing up at her door with a red rose after every one of their wicked fights, wining and dining her till she was blissful again — all sound like? How any girl could catch coping amnesia!

Natalie's story is a little-picture part of this book. The big picture — what this book is really about — is the self-knowledge, information and tools each of us needs to figure out if our boyfriend is right for us or not. Reading the story of Natalie and Ethan, you may have thought, "Yeah, I've been there." So how do you sort through the confusion?

You need a "bar." Think of your bar as something like the one in high jump; only your boyfriend has to clear this one for you to let him into your life in any serious way. How to set your bar correctly, according to how you expect your boy-friend to treat you — anyone to treat you, for that matter — is also what this book is about. Without knowing enough about who she is and what she needs, Natalie will dust herself off and be on her merry way to dating another frog. She could end up in a life of struggling with her own self-worth and settling for unmet needs. Before she even thinks about going out with another guy, she has to realize that she can, and must, create a beautiful life for herself. This book will show you how Natalie goes about doing so — and how you can too.

Let's define a beautiful life. It's the life you've always dreamed of, where you wake up every morning excited about the coming day, where you feel yourself grow happy, where you can fix difficulties that once appeared too big to over-come. A beautiful life is not a fairy tale in which a fairy godmother comes along and makes wonderful things happen. You have to build your own beautiful life, first by becoming familiar with yourself, then by using that self-knowledge to figure out what you need, and finally by making the right choices to get those needs met. The path toward a beautiful life begins with understanding yourself and your needs so that later you'll be able to choose a guy who will help you to meet them.

Childhood fairy tales rarely happen in real life. So build your own fairy tale. In this one, you get to live a life in which your needs truly are met, and since this is a story about Princes and Frogs, you end up living happily ever after with your Prince. How ever long happily ever after is these days? Knowing and respecting yourself will let you identify your *needs* and then make smart *choices* to get those needs met. Making smart choices can bring wonderful *consequences*. Needs, choices, consequences — this process is your learning loop.

In fairy tales, the heroine takes a journey, making marvel-ous and speedy progress, ending up at happily-ever-after. This character gets manipulated by at least one villain who tries to stop her from reaching her goal. We all encounter Frogs who thwart our progress toward self-fulfillment and happily-ever-after. The villain fails because the character is helped out by strange coincidences, like being in the right place at the right time or having the answer she needed right under her nose.

When you become good at using the information and tools in this book, you'll be the character in the fairy tale who gets to make speedy progress toward the happy ending that is possible. We're all characters in our own personal stories. As we move through our stories, we can be helped along by something that's been under our noses all along: self-respect.

We're all pretty clear on the basic rules of respect — to respect our own and others' belongings, for example. What we're not clear on is how to respect ourselves and others while getting our needs met, and how to get others to do the same. Self-respect will help you to develop great "filtering skills"— skills that enable you to recognize and reject a Frog, and recognize, accept and build a relationship with a Prince.

This book will provide you with a set of "dating beliefs" that will show you how to make smart choices in your relationships. Even if you have lots of dating experience, the beginning of any relationship is like the entrance to a maze. We make our way through the maze by making choices, seldom knowing where those choices will take us. When you understand the differences between life with a Prince and life with a Frog, you'll be able to set your own bar correctly, using information from these dating beliefs. Setting your bar will help you make better, more deliberate choices. Choices lead to consequences. By looking carefully at your choices, both good and bad, and linking them to their consequences, you can avoid becoming lost in the maze — lost in your love and in your life.

Since any guy is going to have both Prince and Frog traits, it's hard to decide if your own boyfriend is one or the other. You too might have been thrilled to meet Ethan. At some point, though, maybe when Ethan accused Natalie of wanting to sleep with Tim, you may have said to yourself, "Frog alert! Dump him — he's a jerk!" Wouldn't it be lovely if you could do the same in your own relationship — be certain about whether to stay or go, able to make a decision based on any of your little-picture Frog experiences? Of course, it's easier to see what's wrong with a relationship from the outside; Meghan knew Ethan was a Frog, and she told Natalie to break up with him. When you're in the relationship, it's much harder — sometimes impossible — to see what's wrong and to know what to do about it.

Wouldn't it be lovely if you could be certain about whether to stay or go? Fairy tale girls make it to happily-ever-after, helped out not only by strange coincidences but also by magical incidents like the appearance of a fairy godmother or a yellow-brick road to guide them along their way. You too deserve a fairy godmother of sorts. How about a tool, like a Prince/Frog List to help you see the big picture of your relationship, to understand the good and bad of your relationship even though you're in it!

You deserve to have your needs met — we all do — and to find someone who adds to your happiness. When you find the guy whose needs you're driven to meet and who's driven to meet your needs — who you like and who likes you — you'll find love and grow happy. He'll be a guy you enjoy hanging out and doing things with. When you're alone, you'll feel good — truly good — about yourself and him and the relationship. You deserve to live your life with a Prince.

How do you come to believe deep down inside that you deserve a Prince? In the next chapter you'll take the first step that leads to the fairy tale that's possible — the one you build yourself.

ONE : a beautiful life

$\mathcal{In}$ our dreams, our Prince is a handsome guy who treats us like a Princess. He escorts us to dazzling balls and dances us into the night. He shows us off to his royal friends and to his mother, the Queen. He makes sure that he satisfies our every want and meets our every need. So why is it that most of us don't end up with a guy like the Prince of our dreams?

We don't choose one!

To choose a Prince, you need to believe that you deserve one. And to feel you deserve one, and then go out and choose him, you must first respect yourself. Respecting yourself is not easy when disrespect is thrown at you by all kinds of people — perhaps even your boyfriend. Learning how to respect yourself and to apply self-respect in your life is a long journey. But the farther you travel, making deliberate choices, the easier the journey gets. And the rewards along the way — including choosing your Prince and living happily ever after — are more than worth the effort.

know and respect yourself

As Natalie becomes more familiar with herself by taking a close look at her traits and her interests, she'll take the first

19

steps toward developing her filtering skills, the very skills *you* need to recognize, accept and build a relationship with a Prince. Even more importantly, by working to become familiar with herself, Natalie will develop more self-respect. She'll also begin to draw respect from others, including boyfriends. Getting to know yourself will give you the same great results.

Some get-to-know-yourself exercises will help you start becoming familiar with who you are. Keeping what you like about yourself and changing what you don't — developing new habits, in other words — is one way to self-respect. There's a big reward for completing this self-examination: when you know and like yourself, you'll choose what's good for you, what will help you get to a beautiful life. Meeting your own needs is another way to respect yourself.

You can really get to know yourself by taking a close look at your traits and then deciding what you like and dislike, what you want to keep and what you want to get rid of. A word of caution: when examining your traits, you mustn't beat yourself up over what you think are negative ones. We all have some! Having a trait that you don't like — that you think is bad — doesn't mean you're a bad person. Everybody has warts; even people you think are perfect.

Below is a list of traits. Think about each one and whether or not it applies to you. First, accept your positive traits and allow yourself to feel proud of them. Recognizing that you are thoughtful or unselfish, for example, will help you like yourself more. And when other people acknowledge your positive traits, accept their praise graciously. Instead of saying "I am not…" followed by an embarrassed giggle, try saying, "Thanks. I hadn't thought of myself in that way" or "I'm happy you feel that way." Second, you must "own" your negative traits — you must recognize and accept them the same way you did your positive traits. If the trait applies to you, put an "X" beside it. It's important to be honest; after all, you're the one getting the reward.

i am . . .

○ Moody	○ Even-tempered	○ Daring
○ Outgoing	○ Shy	○ Easygoing
○ Critical	○ Demanding	○ Outspoken
○ Patient	○ Excitable	○ Sociable
○ Funny	○ Enthusiastic	○ Affectionate
○ Selfish	○ Unselfish	○ Thoughtful
○ Stubborn	○ Confident	○ Opinionated
○ Generous	○ Quiet	○ Open-minded
○ Organized	○ Controlling	○ Focused
○ Popular	○ Honest	○ Assertive
○ Energetic	○ Lazy	○ Jealous
○ Creative	○ Passionate	○ Courageous
○ Sweet	○ Kind	○ Sensitive
○ Aggressive	○ Frustrated	○ Nice

Now you've chosen the traits that describe you — or so you think! Take a moment to accept and own all the positive and negative traits that you believe apply to you. The next step is to ask someone who values you (like a best friend) to take a blank copy of the same list and check off the traits she thinks apply to you. Ask her to be 100-percent honest. Tell her she's helping you meet a very important need.

If Natalie asked herself "Who am I?" her perspective would be from the inside out. If she were to ask Meghan "Who am I?" her perspective would be from the outside in. For all of us, there are gaps between who we think we are and who others think we are. You need both your own and others' perspectives to see your positive and negative traits clearly.

When your friend has finished, compare lists. Is there a difference between the traits she picked and those you picked? I bet there is. Say you put an "X" beside "Unselfish," but your best friend put one beside "Selfish." What to do?

Being able to have respectful conversations with others is a necessary condition for getting what you need and want in life. So ask your girlfriend to give you examples of when she thinks you were being selfish. During that conversation make sure you listen to her while she's explaining her perspective.

If you listen, it will be easier for you to get what you need: greater familiarity with yourself. Your friend will also get what she needs: for you to be respectful of her. After all, you asked her to do this.

Find out if you are respectful in conversations with others by answering the following questions:

1) Do you listen to the other person's point of view? Do you know what the word "listening" really means? When you're having a heart-to-heart with your girlfriend, do you:

- look at her when she's talking?
- allow her to finish her sentences without interruption?
- listen to her tone as well as her words?
- remind yourself not to judge her while she's talking?
- ask her to clarify what you don't understand?

Listening to the perspective of others helps you to get the information you need to make smart choices for yourself. Good listening skills are a shortcut to the fairy tale that is possible. If you answer "Yes" to most things on that list, you're *really* listening; if not, you're likely to miss information about why your girlfriend chose the traits she did. This information is important because you're going to use it to make smart choices.

You're respecting the other person when you listen without judgement to what he or she is saying, meeting that person's need to be heard. If you do judge, you'll become distracted and you won't know why she thinks this way; your own need to be clear and not confused will not be met. If your girlfriend's examples aren't exactly what you expected, you may feel a little angry and hurt. Even if you don't agree, you need to understand why she thinks the way she does.

Maybe your girlfriend's definition of "selfish" includes a mistaken belief. Maybe she gave you examples of situations where you needed to take care of yourself first. Putting your needs first might sound selfish, but it isn't always! If your girlfriend nearly always puts other people's feelings and needs ahead of her own just to avoid being selfish, it may be that she doesn't know how to respect herself. It's possible that she acts unselfishly because (consciously or not) she thinks that acts of kindness will cause others to like her. Being unselfish and helping others is important, but you shouldn't have to sacrifice your own needs in the process — at least not all the time.

2) Are you able to listen to points of view with which you disagree without reacting emotionally?

Practice over and over again listening without panicking. We've all been known to butt in, not letting the other person finish her sentence, or to change the subject or even to walk away in anger. Try instead to look at her examples of your selfishness from her perspective, not from your own. Take her example of how you acted selfishly and imagine if someone had acted that way to you. Would you see them as acting selfishly?

Often when we don't agree with another person's point of view (especially when it's critical of us), we feel we have to defend our own perspective. It feels strange to say "Good point" or "You're right" when you don't want what someone is saying to be true, let alone out in the open!

If our emotions get involved — and they usually do — any conversation can turn into an argument. You might feel like interrupting your friend to defend yourself or to attack her point of view. Or does "attacking her point of view" actually mean attacking her? Say you counter with something like "Well, what about how *critical* you are?" To prove your point, you bring up her recent criticisms of your boyfriend. What have you just done? You've undermined the whole point to having the discussion: to learn why your best friend thinks you're selfish. Her criticisms of your boyfriend have nothing to do with this exercise.

Say your best friend gives you examples of when you were truly being selfish or self-centered, not considering someone else's feelings and needs when you should have. What if you did not like how the world saw you from the outside? You might decide you don't want to be selfish anymore. Accept yourself as being selfish by removing the "X" beside "Unselfish" on your own list of traits and placing it next to "Selfish." Own that trait. Then by using your friend's examples, work at changing how you choose to act in those situations. The change will occur over time, because in order to turn a new trait into a habit, you must be disciplined and work at the change for a while.

This kind of change is an example of respecting yourself. You owned up to a quality you did not like and did something about it. Remember that once you've identified this wart — and others — even if you can't change it, you must accept yourself. We're not perfect; each of us is selfish sometimes. But the key is to work at being unselfish more often. You'll become more genuinely beautiful by working on yourself from the inside out than you will by brushing your hair or putting on makeup.

It's easy to believe that if you looked like a top model or a movie star or a pop singer — Presto! — you'd be living a beautiful life. But real life isn't like that. Just look at all the models and celebrities and singers whose lives are disasters; the gossip magazines are full of young women who don't know themselves and choose Frogs over and over again. What leads to a beautiful life is not good looks or celebrity or money. It is investing time and energy into changing what you cannot comfortably accept about yourself, as in the example above. How much time and energy? Well, at the very least as much as you're willing to invest in meeting your boyfriend's needs.

In addition to examining your traits, finding out what you enjoy and what's special about you also helps you to get to know yourself. Have you been complimented for doing a good job on something? Do you have a wonderful way with small children or old people or animals that you could develop into an exciting and rewarding career? What was/is your favorite subject in school? Which subject did/do you get great marks in? Every one of us has talent or ability in some area. Natalie has a real gift for doing detailed research, thinking logically and presenting a convincing argument. She watches *Law & Order* and *CSI* faithfully and probably will make a great lawyer. When we find and start to develop our special ability, we take a huge step toward not only respecting ourselves but also getting respect from others.

Continue the process of finding yourself by looking at what you like to do. What hobbies and activities do you enjoy because they make you feel good? Some of us like physical activity because it gives us a great rush and keeps us in shape and because we're good at it. Others prefer creative or artistic pursuits because they give us a feeling of accomplishment or serve as a wonderful release from the tensions of study or work. Spend time thinking about the activities or hobbies you like. Circle the activities that you would like to do more often:

GENERAL ACTIVITIES: Fine food, Dancing, Walking, Shopping, Travel, Driving, Flying, Camping, Playing games, Boating, Movies, Music, TV.

TEAM SPORTS: Baseball, Volleyball, Hockey, Soccer.

INDIVIDUAL SPORTS: Aerobics, Gymnastics, Ice skating, Skiing, Tennis, Diving, Martial arts, Bicycling, RollerBlading, Jogging, Swimming, Hiking, Horseback riding.

HOBBIES/INTERESTS: Sketching, Painting, Reading, Poetry, Politics, Researching special interests, Sewing, Writing, Ceramics, Volunteer work, Joining groups/clubs where you share special interests with others.

What does this exercise tell you? That your life is chock full of activities and hobbies and you couldn't possibly fit one more into your schedule? That you're interested in lots of things and just don't have the time to pursue them as actively as you'd like? That you should choose to do more of the activities that you like and that, if you really tried, you could fit them into your schedule? That you don't have many activities or hobbies at all, that you're too busy hanging out with your boyfriend and doing things he likes to do? If your answer to this last question is yes, you might want to make some changes. Start by choosing to do more of the activities you like and developing more hobbies. Your reward: you'll feel better and you'll be less and less in need of your friends' approval.

This exercise may help you identify what you're especially good at; if so, you've taken another step toward closing the gap between who you are and who you can become. Meeting a need in your life is a goal, and you must set your goals with as much knowledge and honesty about who you are as possible. For example, don't aim to become a lawyer if you quit the book club because you didn't enjoy reading and the debating club because you hated arguing your points. Setting goals and then changing them later is okay; we all grow and change. It's important to start somewhere and to include what you find out about yourself in your choices.

what's a need?

We all want lots of things to take care of ourselves and others and to make us grow happy. When we get a need met, we usually feel happy — or no longer wanting. When we can't get what we need, we feel that something is missing or something isn't right.

When you're hungry, you eat, fulfilling a basic need. Simple, right? Not always. Because a good or bad consequence follows *how* you choose to meet that need. For instance, if you were on a diet yet you chose a triple hot-fudge sundae, the consequence would be disappointment in yourself. Now think about the bigger picture. Suppose your blue dress didn't fit, so you decided to lose some weight. After you wolfed down that sundae, you would have felt disappointed in yourself because you'd moved away from getting yourself back into that blue dress. You had two needs: the need to eat and the need to feel better by losing weight and fitting into your blue dress. Satisfying both needs meant choosing something healthier than a sundae. In the end, choosing the sundae meant satisfying one need at the expense of the other. Would understanding this simple consequence help you choose differently next time? Control of the learning loop — how you respond to the needs-choices-consequences sequence — is entirely in your hands.

What if a doctor tells you that you're at risk of developing diabetes unless you lose 50 pounds, and you ignore her advice? In this case, the consequence — diabetes — is very different from disappointment. Consciously or not, you'd be choosing not to take care of yourself. Making the choice not to take care of ourselves is one way we don't respect ourselves.

You've already started to become familiar with yourself, and this process helps you to understand what you need. Identifying your needs will lead you to make good choices in love and in life. Being familiar with yourself, keeping your eye on the big picture of your beautiful life and learning from experiencing the consequences — good and bad — in the learning loop will help you make better choices. And making better choices, time after time, is the goal in the game of life!

what needs are you responsible to meet for yourself?

Can you list all the needs you'd have to meet each day to be happy and make progress toward your goals in life? Identifying your needs may appear complicated and difficult, but it isn't.

There are four basic groups of needs: emotional, physical, intellectual and lifestyle. Knowledge of these needs will help you make better choices in life and in love. You're responsible for understanding what your own needs are and then seeing that they get met.

In the big picture there are three ways of getting your needs met:

- Meeting your needs yourself
- Having your needs met by others
- Meeting the needs of others

In this chapter, we're looking at what needs you're responsible to meet for yourself. Although this may sound selfish, understanding your own needs and how to get them met *before* considering someone else's feelings is actually *unselfish*. When your own needs are met, your happiness, confidence and sense of self will be strong, and you'll more easily be able to give others what they seek from you. So remember: work to understand your needs and how to get them met first. Natalie was so busy trying to meet Ethan's needs that she never stopped to consider her own. Until she starts to make deliberate choices to get to know what her needs are, and then actively tries to meet these needs, she won't love herself. Until she makes those choices, she won't really understand how to love Ethan. Worse, she won't really understand whether or not Ethan loves her. This same approach will make you a strong and respectful relationship partner. We're in much a better position to understand, respect and meet the needs of others when we've already done this for ourselves.

There are several *emotional* needs that any girl is responsible to meet: to become familiar with herself, to accept herself, to forgive herself and to value herself. Becoming familiar with yourself helps you make choices that are true to who you are and help move you toward who you want to become. When you know more about who you are and act like the person you know yourself to be, you'll meet another need: to accept yourself. If you've accepted yourself, you'll come to understand that you're not perfect and you'll forgive yourself for not always meeting your own expectations or for any honest mistakes you've made. Building self-worth begins with knowing and accepting who you are.

There are two *physical* needs that any girl is responsible to meet: to notice and to desire. To notice means to become aware of your beauty and to have a positive sense of your physical body. This awareness leads you to appreciate every part of your body when you see it in the mirror, not just when you're on the way to a party. To really appreciate your body you must take care of your physical health; proper care includes exercising regularly, paying attention to diet and hygiene and so on. To desire means we long for physical touch, the sharing of physical affection with others. Giving and receiving hugs or even taking care of your pet can meet this need.

There are several *intellectual* needs that any girl is responsible to meet: to stay interested and challenged, and to listen to, understand, support and be proud *of* herself. You will meet your need to be interested by staying connected to the world around you. One way of keeping this connection is through paying attention to current events by regularly watching the news and discussing it with your friends and family. Each of us needs to be clear and not confused, to be curious and to understand how we fit into the world, both in terms of what people expect from us — at work, at school, in the family and so forth — and of how we build our goals and dreams. You'll meet your need to be challenged by exploring the issue of "What I want to do with my life," whether it's attending university and studying for a professional career, getting a diploma at a business college, becoming an artist or a writer or following any other path. We all need to feel that our minds are being put to good and rewarding use. We all have the answers inside us, so listen carefully to yourself and you'll choose the right career for you. You'll meet your need to be proud *of* yourself by creating dreams and exploring ways to achieve them — supporting yourself in your own efforts.

Finally, there are several *lifestyle* needs that any girl is responsible to meet to create or maintain her beautiful life: to be safe, capable, in control, alive, important, pleased, helpful and free. To be safe, a girl needs to protect herself from physical harm; she must also protect herself from financial harm by making and saving enough money to pay her bills and stay out of debt. Building herself a beautiful life will enable her to take care of her needs (like food and rent) and her wants (like facials and purses) and to do the things she enjoys, meeting her needs to feel capable, competent and in control of her life.

Actively working to meet your needs will make you feel as if a door has opened. You'll feel more energetic, able to tackle your troubles, thus meeting your need to feel alive. Sounds like a beautiful life, right? When you see yourself trying to meet your own needs — being helpful to yourself– you'll feel important to yourself. Making sure you schedule in treats, hobbies or enjoyable activities will meet your need to please yourself. We all have a need to be free, or uncontrolled, and you'll meet this need by closing the gaps between what you want to do and what you actually do, and by taking care of yourself first.

your to do list

Using a To Do List to close the gaps between your current activities and what you want to do in your life is a shortcut to the fairy tale that's possible. To get your needs met, make a To Do List; this will get you closer to the life you want. A To Do List is like a grocery list, with the sort of organizing that goes into a school planner. Some of the items on your To Do List may appear only once. When you've completed the task, cross it off and move on. New items will appear on tomorrow's list. Routine items like "Walk the dog" or "Phone Meghan" appear almost every day on Natalie's list. Most of the time, you don't have to write down routine items; they're a part of your mental To Do List. Only when you've strayed from your basic routine and want to get back into it would you put these items back on your written To Do List.

Every girl's To Do List is uniquely designed to work for her. Your list might be very different from your best friend's, although some of the items may be the same. A To Do List consists of a woman's deliberate choices to do what she enjoys, to take care of herself and others and to achieve her dreams. Here's a sample of a To Do List for one day.

elizabeth's to do list
today's date

- Coffee with quartet members (8:15)
- Lunch with Gwen at Gino's (12:30)
- See Professor Davies about recital (2:30?)
- Practise new piece (for at least two hours!!!)
- Pick up brother at karate (5:00)
- Call Michael about Saturday's party
- Call Sydney to check if she's going to aerobics class in the morning

From her To Do List, we can see that Elizabeth is meeting lots of her own needs as well as meeting the needs of others. Her list shows that she's working hard every day to play music, stay fit and have fun as well as being there for her best friend Gwen and others. Create and manage your own To Do List and you'll get a wonderful feeling of satisfaction. Make deliberate choices to actively work toward your dreams and you will experience success, which will help you to believe in yourself and build confidence so that you can accomplish almost anything that's important to you.

the learning loop: an illustration
If you're familiar enough with yourself and truly understand your needs, you can use the learning loop (needs-choices-con-

sequences) to figure out what you want to do in your life. This loop enables you to meet your need to be clear and not confused. Here's an example of how you might use it to move closer to your beautiful life. Say you get great marks in science and math, and you're also interested in the well-being of animals. Watching TV shows about abused and neglected animals has made you think you might like to become a veterinarian. Such a career would allow you to care for suffering creatures and at the same time meet your need to be safe in a career that gives you financial security. You could test this need and then go about meeting it by adding an important item to your To Do List —"Volunteer or get a part-time job at a veterinary clinic"— to check out whether becoming a vet might be a good choice for you.

Suppose, after working at the clinic for a while, you experienced a real connection to the animals and the staff. The passion you thought you had turned out to be real; in fact, it was even stronger than you'd imagined. You also discovered that you had a lot in common with the people at the clinic — you fit right in. Once, you even really helped an animal in need. Helping people and animals made you feel good about yourself. You learned a lot from the experience, and it left you feeling you'd done something of real value.

In this example, you identified a need, made a choice that allowed you to explore that need, then experienced good consequences. The learning loop worked as it should. You identified a passion and chose to explore that passion. The consequence confirmed that your need was real and that you were happy caring for animals. You learned about yourself, your abilities and how good it feels to use your interests to discover what you want to do. What if your experience confirmed that your need was not real? You'd still have experienced a good consequence. You now know more about yourself, your needs and how to get them met, all because you identified a need, made a deliberate choice and then paid attention to the consequences. Voilà: the learning loop.

self-respect and meeting needs

Let's look at Natalie again and see how she aligned who she was with what she did. When she met Ethan, her dream was to become a lawyer and she was working toward this goal at college. In her relationship, however, she started making choices in her day-to-day life that weren't based on who she thought she was or what she wanted to do. Now, if you're thinking, "Yeah, but she had already started to slack off: she found school boring, and it was while she was skipping class that she met Ethan," you'd be right. Even before she met him, she was having a hard time committing to her dream, finding it hard to focus and do the work that would get her into law school. Meeting Ethan just made this worse. In the storyline, she makes a ton of honest mistakes: heart-over-head choices to fix her anxious Ethan feelings, jumping through hoops like a clumsy ballerina to meet his needs, paying little attention to her own needs. The gap between what she wanted to do and what she actually did got bigger.

Natalie let her relationship consume her life instead of making sure that it was part of her To Do List. By not following through with the choices she made — to become a lawyer, to be a best friend to Meghan — she failed to keep building herself a beautiful life.

Natalie needs to focus on her own To Do List. One of the items on the list could be to work on her feelings with Ethan, but she can't allow this item to squeeze out tasks that mattered before she met him, such as attending classes and keeping plans with Meghan. Getting lost is easy when you make heart-over-head choices. Holding on to her self-respect would have led her to make different choices, such as not putting his needs before her own — thereby pretty much giving up her own life.

If Natalie had all along been using a To Do List, the List would have changed over time. Items like "Call Meghan re: workout time," "Study for criminology test," and "Pick up journals for sociology paper" would have been replaced with "Ethan…," "Ethan…" and "Ethan…."

Natalie's heart was broken and maybe your own heart has been broken, too. Throughout the book you'll encounter a number of "heart-saving shortcuts." These are ways of *avoiding* a broken heart that have been learned the hard way by many women before you.

♡ HEART-SAVING SHORTCUT: Most of the girls in childhood fairy tales were lost in their lives, in miserable situations that didn't meet their needs. Yet somehow, magically, they each ended up with a Prince. Remember that life doesn't actually happen this way — that's why childhood stories are called fairy tales! In real life, if you're lost in your life you won't choose a Prince.

After you've read this chapter and completed the exercises, you may notice that you're feeling, looking and sleeping better, waking more refreshed and energetic. You'll be less irritable and impatient with friends and family, you'll be stronger and more decisive and you'll find you can get done what you need to.

By looking at your traits, at what you like and how you communicate with others, you get to know yourself better and develop self-respect. As a result of changes you've made, you'll also find that others begin to respect you more. You'll worry less about making a good impression and you'll be less tempted to make up stories about yourself, because when you know and value yourself, you feel comfortable with who you are. When you make better choices, the gap between who you *say* you are — the type of person you *claim* to be — and who you *really* are almost disappears. The new you might find that some of the people you've been associating with no longer appeal to you. Life is a mirror: what you seek in others should be a reflection of who you are.

♡ HEART-SAVING SHORTCUT: If you ever find yourself having a conversation with your girlfriend trying to figure out a situation and you hear yourself saying (with no shame or guilt, but simply as a matter of fact): "Well, maybe that's because I can be a little controlling in situations like this," you go, girl!

Take a look around and notice who your friends are, who comes and goes, how things change on the outside as you do more work on the inside. Making better choices encourages you to be around people who also respect themselves and are comfortable with who they are. Your former friends may think you're a snob or a traitor. You're not. You've simply recognized that choosing villains in your story only adds to your struggles. Choosing Frogs makes life harder. Just doing what we have to do to meet our own needs is hard enough.

To choose a Prince, you must be building a beautiful life for yourself. If, like Natalie, you're bored and unhappily waiting to be rescued, no relationship — with a Prince or a Frog — is going to make you happy. The self-respect you establish on the way to building your beautiful life will give you excellent filtering skills. Your newfound self-respect may actually cause some guys to steer clear of you. They're doing you a favor! Good riddance to Frogs! The guys with *character* will stick around, and it's among these guys that you just might find your Prince.

What do we mean by character? In the next chapter, we'll find out.

TWO: *shopping*

The word "complete" describes what it feels like to live in a beautiful life. In the big picture there are three ways to meet each need. If you're truly in love with a guy, for example, you love yourself, you love him and he loves you in turn. You can be sure that if each need in a relationship isn't met in all three ways, you won't be using the word "complete" to describe your life. We've already discussed the first way: meeting your own needs. In this chapter we'll talk about the other two ways: how Ethan should meet Ella's needs and how she should meet his.

getting your needs met

Enjoy shopping? Well, think of life as one big shopping experience. We all shop at the Meet-Your-Needs Mall every day, adding to our beautiful lives, and we're all responsible for choosing what we want. When you shop for clothes, you choose items — pants, blouses, shoes, underwear, coats — from different stores. When you try to get your needs met by others — parents, friends or guys — think of yourself as shopping at different boutiques (your boyfriend's, your best friend's, your mom's).

Every time you close the gap between what you think meets a need and what *actually* meets a need, you become more familiar with yourself. One part of learning about your needs is information; the other part comes from experience. To illustrate this point, let's take a quick shopping trip. On this trip we'll compare getting what you think meets a need (a silver medal) with getting what really does meet that need (which feels like winning a gold).

Say you're invited to a party. You want to look great, to meet your need to be noticed. You feel you have nothing nice to wear, so you go shopping. At the store, you pick out different styles of tops, all of them black. (You believe black is slimming.) In the change room, you choose a black top you feel good in, and you go ahead and buy it. Shortly after this shopping experience, a girlfriend convinces you to try on her new pink top. You're shocked to discover the color pink was invented just for you. You felt attractive in the black top, but now you realize it only gets a silver medal. The pink top makes you feel incredibly sexy, so it wins a gold. You just learned that if you want to meet your need to be noticed — to feel fabulous and get heads turning your way — you'll get a pink top.

Of course, this experience wasn't planned; it just happened. You close the gap between what you think met a need and what really meets it by becoming more familiar with yourself. You adjust your self-knowledge and then use it to make more deliberate choices. Now you know to buy pink tops instead of black ones to meet your need to be noticed. When you experience the true fulfillment of a need, you store the knowledge of how it felt. And you try to recapture the feeling in other situations.

Take Ella. Her new boyfriend Ethan drives her home. She thinks this is sweet; it's something a lot of guys wouldn't think of. But she can't get out of her mind what her ex-boyfriend used to do. So one night, as they pull up at her house, she has a little chat with Ethan.

ETHAN: (Leaning over to kiss her) Good night, baby.

ELLA: (Kisses him) You know how you always drive me home?

ETHAN: I just wanna be sure you're safe.

ELLA: Well, I think it's really sweet. (She laughs)

ETHAN: Yeah, well, any guy should do that.

ELLA: Do you know what would make me even happier?

ETHAN: What, baby?

ELLA: I'd so love it if you'd wait until I get in the door before you take off. Do you think I'm being demanding here?

ETHAN: (Laughing) I'm going to sit back and enjoy watching you from behind.

Ella gets out of the car and walks happily to her door. She turns to blow him a kiss before he pulls away from the curb. How easy that was! All she had to do was ask Ethan and she got her need met.

using character to get your needs met

Each of us makes different choices in how to get our needs met. Why? Because we all have different beliefs that lead us to act in certain ways. We're also influenced by a society that promotes instant gratification, so we look for shortcuts to get our needs met. How do you get your needs met from others? Do you practise *character* when getting them met?

Character is three things: saying what you mean, doing what you say and using your beliefs to choose right from wrong. If you try to build character in yourself, you'll respect others. The combination of self-respect and respect for others is a great foundation on which to build a good relationship with a boyfriend, a best friend or anyone else.

"Do I say what I mean?" is really about honesty. Being honest with others means you give accurate information about how you think and feel. It means you're upfront about what you want and why. And it means you don't lie for any reason, whether to get your own way or to avoid hurting others.

You might believe you sometimes need to lie because telling the truth would only hurt another person's feelings. But suppose your girlfriend gets a bad haircut and she loves it. She asks what you think. You have a choice: lie and tell her it's fabulous too or tell the truth and say you don't think it suits her. What are the consequences of each choice? If you lie, she'll probably keep getting awful haircuts. Perhaps others will talk, and laugh, behind her back.

If you tell the truth, perhaps she'll be hurt. How hurt depends on how you tell her. After she hears your opinion, she'll ask for others' opinions. It will soon become clear to her that the haircut doesn't suit her and she'll change hairdressers. So it's a mistaken belief to think you're being kind or thoughtful by lying to her about anything.

People lie for all kinds of reasons. We tell white lies to avoid hurting others' feelings. We tell sugar-coated lies to get what we want, to avoid doing something or to prevent an argument. And we tell lies to impress people. Lying to get what we want or need is *manipulation*. Say you want a ride from your boyfriend because it's raining and you feel lazy. He's at his house and feels lazy too. When you ask him to pick you up, he says, "Can't you take the bus?" Instead of telling him you feel lazy (and giving him the chance to pick you up just to make you happy), you make up a reason — a lie — like "I hurt my ankle." Or you add some sugar words before you ask for a ride, using his favorite nickname and telling him you love him (even if you don't). This is manipulation. By the way, it's perfectly okay to add sugar words, to be playful and teasing ("Please, baby, pick me up. You know I'd do it for you"), but only if you really do love the guy, in which case the words are just adding to his happiness and his picking you up in the rain is adding to yours.

When you say what you feel and think, you're building self-worth, one sentence at a time. Telling lies, like everything you do, has consequences. Your self-worth will shrink when you lie because lying will make you feel like a big faker. Worse, lying can reinforce the fear that we can never be accepted for who we *really* are or for what we *really* think.

Lying usually is about taking shortcuts to get your pet wants satisfied. Lying also indicates how much you value yourself. Maybe you don't believe someone would value you enough to do what you ask just because doing it adds to your happiness. You shouldn't have to lie to get what you want. If your request is reasonable and your boyfriend loves and respects you, he'll be happy to give you what you want, if he can. If you lie to friends not only to avoid hurting their feelings but also to avoid a hard conversation where conflict may result, you're actually not respecting them or yourself much. They'll keep doing things you know they shouldn't because you never tell them what you really feel and think. If you value them, you'll tell them the truth — kindly and gently, but honestly. If they value and respect you, they'll understand that your honesty comes from your respect for them. If they're upset with your honesty, the problem is theirs, not yours.

Finally, if you have to lie to impress a potential boyfriend or friend because you feel he or she cannot accept you as you are, maybe that person is not the one for you. If you've worked hard at finding, knowing and respecting yourself, others will respect you and be impressed by you. There'll be no need to lie or make up stories.

The next character question —"Do I do what I say I will?"— is about keeping commitments, to yourself and others. When you know yourself and respect yourself, you'll usually follow through on commitments. You're self-disciplined and dependable; people know they can count on you. When you want to make a change in your life or develop a new habit, you do. When you promise your girlfriend you'll keep her secrets, you do. When you tell your boyfriend you'll call him after class, you do. You don't make promises or commitments simply to get your needs met. You're not the kind of person who says, "Meghan, I'll help you with your criminology project if you lend me your psychology notes" and then, once your needs are met, you forget all about hers. So much for respecting Meghan.

The final character question—"Do you use your beliefs and values to understand the difference between right and wrong?"—is about the beliefs that guide us, and how they help us determine the difference between right and wrong. Gossiping about your girlfriend in order to gain popularity is a good example of compromising your sense of right and wrong. What about when, in the Introduction, Elizabeth didn't keep what Natalie told her in confidence; she let slip details of Natalie's love story to Tim, who told Ethan. Was Elizabeth being disrespectful to Natalie? Was Natalie being disrespectful to Ethan?

There is a gray area between talking behind someone's back respectfully and doing so disrespectfully. You can still talk about someone with respect when you're trying to understand yourself, a situation or someone else better. For example, are you frustrated with your boyfriend because he keeps doing whatever it is you've asked him not to do? Or have you had a huge fight with your boyfriend and need to talk about it with a trusted friend? In both of these cases there is a common thread: you have to get your feelings off your chest—in confidence—to help you meet your need to be clear and not confused. So it looks like Natalie's off the hook.

What about Elizabeth? It's disrespectful to talk about someone when the conversation is not about trying to understand yourself, a situation or someone else better. For example, you might be fishing for gossip — if you give a little, you get a little. Whether Elizabeth gave information to Tim to get Ethan information for Natalie or to get closer to Tim, it's never okay to break a confidence. Natalie valued Elizabeth, yet Elizabeth didn't respect her. What about you? Maybe someone's stopped you from getting your way. You feel hurt and, either consciously or unconsciously, you want to vilify that person to anyone who will listen. Natalie built Ella a nasty reputation after Ella started to go out with Ethan, even though Ella didn't break any girl codes. You might have talked like this about one of your own girlfriends because she didn't give you what you wanted, didn't agree with your opinion or failed to invite you to a party at her house. And if you later run into the friend you were talking about and, feeling better, you give her a big kiss, tell her how wonderful she is and then make plans to do something next week, that's called being two-faced. So much for your girly-girl strategy to get her snubbed!

Suppose after reading the section on respectful conversations in Chapter One, you agreed with the points made and took them on as beliefs. Yet you recognize that you can still butt in or even become rather vicious, attacking with insinuations and subtle accusations when conversations escalate into arguments. This means that you're finding it hard in everyday life to use this belief about respectful conversations. It's only practice that reduces the gap between believing and doing. So recognize what's going on and keep practising. You'll get there.

♡ HEART-SAVING SHORTCUT: Disrespectful conversations can include speaking in loud and angry tones or calling someone nasty names, like "slut," "bitch," or "asshole." Then there are completely unacceptable acts, like pushing or hitting someone. You can't have a respectful conversation with anyone who acts like this. Don't even try!

your boyfriend's boutique

Figuring out what you need in life is hard, and figuring out what you need in a boyfriend might be the hardest task of all. If Natalie had been asked what needs she wanted Ethan to meet, she might have found it difficult to answer. She'd never really thought about it.

Just as our shopper chose the black top because she felt comfortable with that choice, you'll probably choose a boyfriend who meets the needs that are familiar to you. Part of the choice you make in boyfriends is going to be based on what needs you know you have, or what needs you've experienced being met or not met.

In the beginning of her relationship with Ethan, Natalie expected few of her needs to get met. Some of her needs — to love, the need for physical affection, the needs to be noticed, to notice, to be desired, to be interested, to be interesting, to please — were being fulfilled. But Ethan was not fulfilling a lot of needs Natalie deserved to get met: the need to be valued, to be forgiven, to have him become familiar with her, to understand her and to please her.

So how do you figure out what you need in a boyfriend? Let's revisit the four needs groups — emotional, physical, intellectual and lifestyle — and see what Ella should be shopping for at Ethan's boutique.

She'd shop to fulfill these emotional needs: to become familiar with Ethan, to accept him, to forgive him and to value him. Drawn into loving him, she'd be crazy about his happiness, which she'd enjoy adding to. She'd want to get to know him (become familiar with him) and then be able to accept him for who he is, as he is, able to forgive him for honest mistakes. Over time she'd grow to value him, be able to tell him what she really feels and thinks.

She'd shop to fulfill these physical needs: to notice and desire. Ethan's looks and that special something about him would have stopped her in her tracks the first night she met him at the beach party; and what she noticed would have stood out in her mind afterward. Ethan would match that picture in her imagination of a ridiculously good-looking guy. She's attracted to guys who are tall and blond. He's both. She'd love how he showed physical affection. He holds her hand — is a hot kisser. She'd become crazy about him; she'd desire him and crave more and more physical affection from him. Nestling in his arms should make her feel warm and desired.

She'd shop to fulfill her intellectual needs. Ella wants to be with a guy she's really interested in. She'd find herself asking Ethan a gazillion questions and she'd listen to every word he said. When he told her his opinion, he'd capture her interest. She'd shop for a guy she understands; she's not looking for someone who, after a conversation, leaves her feeling bewildered or confused. She'd want to be with a guy whose beliefs about the world she could support, whose opinions she could challenge and with whom she could have respectful arguments. She'd seek a guy she was proud to introduce to her friends.

She'd shop to fulfill her lifestyle needs. She'd want to feel alive when they were together, hanging out. She'd seek a guy she wants to please, take care of and be helpful to just because it adds to his happiness. Ethan has interests that are different from hers, and she'd be excited to explore these interests (opening up new areas in her life), meeting her own need to be pleased. She'd not feel she had to manage or fix Ethan's life, because he did such a good job himself, meeting his own need to be free. Of course we all need our boyfriends to be safe from harm and free from pain, so if he makes great choices, she'll get to be his real girlfriend, not his second mother — and she'll be one lucky girlfriend.

meeting your boyfriend's needs

In your own relationship do you really feel valued, accepted, noticed, interesting, understood, supported and so on? Once your needs are getting met, you can safely turn back to the original daisy game: "He loves me, he loves me not?" To answer this, you need to build an understanding of your boyfriend's needs. You might even be able to make a list of the needs your boyfriend is shopping for at your boutique. Can you meet these needs? Does your boutique carry what he's looking for?

Your boyfriend is shopping at your boutique for the same needs as you are at his. He too is looking for someone he can love, accept, notice, desire, be proud of. You get your needs met by meeting his because you feel the effect when any one of his needs gets met. He's attracted to you, he notices you and you see him come alive and light up when he's around you. His happiness and the way he shows it meet your need to be noticed! Let's look at what Ethan should be shopping for at Ella's boutique.

Ella will feel *her* emotional needs met when Ethan shops at her boutique to fulfill his. We all deserve to love and be loved. By meeting Ethan's need to have someone he can love, Ella will get her own need to be loved met. Ethan will show his love to her by becoming familiar with her — her traits, what she likes and what she needs to grow happy in her life. She'll get her need to be accepted met when she feels he knows her and likes what he knows — he's not critical of everything she does and doesn't always try to change the way she does things. Hopefully Ethan knows it's impossible for Ella to be perfect, so he can meet her need to be forgiven for honest mistakes. She'll get her need to be valued met when Ethan trusts her enough to tell her how he feels and thinks — about himself and her.

Ella will feel *her* physical needs met while Ethan shops at her boutique to meet his. Just as Ella needs to have someone she can notice, so does Ethan. By meeting his need to notice, she'll get her own need to be noticed met. A girl doesn't have to look like a movie star or a fashion model. Each of us has our own unique beauty that will bewitch a Prince. If you're the girl for him, he'll notice your beauty. The attention Ethan pays to Ella and his physical affection for her should meet her need to be desired.

Ella will feel *her* intellectual needs met while Ethan shops at her boutique to meet his. When we are attracted to someone, we're going to be curious about them and want to find out as much information as possible about what they think and feel. Ethan's genuine interest in everything about Ella will meet her need to be interesting. Everyone has certain beliefs about how the world works — about what is right and wrong and how relationships work. When Ethan can agree with Ella's beliefs, her need to feel supported will be met, as will his need to support the one he loves. When Ethan doesn't agree, her need to be challenged will be met as she explains her views. Ethan then might move closer to understanding her and to understanding why he believes what he does. In conversations, if Ethan's truly listening, he'll meet her need to be heard and understood. When he asks for her opinion or asks her to advise him on what to do in a situation, he'll meet her need for someone to be proud of her.

Ella will feel *her* lifestyle needs met when Ethan is shopping at her boutique to meet his. As I mentioned earlier, Ella will see him come alive, as when Ethan gets excited while they're making plans to do stuff together. If Ethan feels she's capable and competent, her need to be free will get met. When he tries to meet her needs by including them and prioritizing them in his To Do List, he'll meet her need to feel important. When Ethan helps her with her To Do List — because he needs to help that special someone in his life — he'll meet Ella's need to be helped. We all have a need to please. When

Ethan remembers little details about her favorite food or activity and then includes those in what they do, she'll feel pleased. And he'll have met his need to please her.

♡ HEART-SAVING SHORTCUT: Here's a quick way to find out what needs your boyfriend is shopping for at your store: Ask him what he likes about you. A Prince will most likely answer with what he likes about you as a person — your personality and character qualities — and the needs you meet for him. A Frog will usually answer with only what you do for him, how you meet his needs. Often these are the guys who use currency like fast cars, bling (diamonds and pearls) and expensive dinners to shop at a girl's boutique. Do you know why this guy is investing in you?

needs and pet wants

You're one of a kind. The ways in which you feel your needs should be met are unique to you. What one girl shops for at her boyfriend's boutique can be very different from what another shops for. Say the guy you're going out with spends a lot of time looking through a telescope and studying the stars. If you're also obsessed with stars, the time you spend with him will be fun for both of you. If you're not interested in astronomy, you're likely going to be bored and this guy will not be the Prince you dreamed of. This activity would meet one girl's need to be pleased — to enjoy her activities. For another girl, it wouldn't.

Despite our individuality, we all shop for fulfillment of the same needs. Pet wants, on the other hand, are the ways each individual believes his or her needs should be met. Let's illustrate how a need gets met with the satisfaction of a girl's pet want. To do this we'll use an example of a guy meeting the girl's lifestyle need to feel important. For any girl to get this need met, she must feel that her boyfriend includes her feelings and needs in his choices. One girl might feel important if her boyfriend calls twice a day (pet want), but this kind of attention might drive another girl crazy. Yet another girl might feel important if her boyfriend pays a lot of attention to her while they're out with friends (pet want). Other girls might feel this boyfriend is needy and doesn't give them any space. Funny but true. The satisfaction of many different pet wants could meet this need for you to feel important — your boyfriend canceling his plans so he can visit you instead, for example, because you sprained your ankle, or because you told him you missed him, wanted a hug or were upset.

Any guy would find some of the pet wants above reasonable and others unreasonable. Say you had two pet wants connected to your need to feel important. You wanted your boyfriend to call every day and to cancel his plans and show up when you fancied a hug; your boyfriend might find only the first pet want reasonable. Since he found your second pet want unreasonable, he might refuse to do what you asked. If you could give up this pet want and still respect yourself and grow happy without it, the pet want would be like an extra goodie — great if you can get it, but still okay if you can't. You'll have a variety of pet wants that you'll connect to getting a need met and pet wants that you won't. How we make the connection will be different for each one of us. As you become familiar with yourself, you'll learn what your own unique pet wants are. More importantly, you'll begin to understand which pet wants link to needs and which don't.

Let's take a different look at the link between pet wants and needs. Sometimes pet wants are extra goodies we get by not respecting ourselves. We might think of extra goodies as trivial, yet we know how important they can be. Ever tempted to buy that new pair of shoes you can't afford but *really* want? Well, if you used your rent money to buy the shoes and then couldn't pay your rent (thus not meeting your need to be safe), it would become an unreasonable pet want. Why? Because you gave up self-respect to satisfy it.

meeting one another's needs

When we buy what we need from a store, we consider price: what you pay, or give up, to get what you want. In a relationship, remember, you're shopping to meet needs in the four groups: emotional, physical, intellectual and lifestyle. What you find helps you determine if your boyfriend is the right guy for you. Maybe you won't get all of your pet wants met in a relationship. On your list of pet wants, you'll have some that are really important and others you can live without while still respecting yourself. Every decision you make has a price, a consequence that you have to experience. In a relationship, the price you pay for choosing to stay with your boyfriend might be not getting a pet want satisfied.

Making choices in relationships is about figuring out what you need to be happy; each of us may be willing to pay a different price for happiness. But when we make decisions that ignore our beliefs or do not take into account our own feelings and needs, we're paying a price in self-respect we can't afford.

Shopping involves a simple transaction: you pay for what you want. You're happy; the shop owner is happy. When you shop at your boyfriend's boutique, it's not usually such a simple transaction; you may not both get what you need at the same time. After all, you're shopping for items in all four need groups. And shopping in a relationship is more complicated than in a store because you both have lots of currency options: emotional, physical, intellectual and lifestyle. Conducting transactions in a relationship is more like trade; for example, you might be shopping for fulfillment of *emotional* needs while your boyfriend is shopping to meet his *physical* needs.

Ouch! If you respect yourself, why let a guy shop at your store for physical needs using currencies such as fancy cars or dinners? You should accept only valuable currency — emotional currency, which is a guy being interested in who you are and caring about how you feel. This is the currency a Prince would use in his campaign to win your heart.

(?) BROKEN-HEART SHORTCUT: Let's talk about your va-jay-jay. Often girls use their va-jay-jay just like guys use their wallets, to take shortcuts to getting their needs met. There is a big difference between using a wallet and a va-jay-jay for currency. Which consequence sounds worse to you: a whittled-down bank account or a diminished sense of self-worth? Use your va-jay-jay with feeling and intention. Don't use it for currency to barter for other needs.

How do you go about shopping for fulfillment of your needs at your boyfriend's boutique? How does he shop at yours? Are you both asking with respect for your needs to be met? Or are you demanding? What does either of you do when a need is not met? Do you get nasty and punish the other person? How we choose to get our needs met is important. In a relationship you can't choose what you want and then pay for it with cash or a credit card as you can in a store. You have to ask for what you want and then wait for the yes or no answer. He has to do the same. After all, the person being asked to satisfy the pet want is the one who gets to decide if it's reasonable or not.

There are different ways in which you can get your boyfriend to meet your needs. You can be respectful and use character, or you can say things that you don't mean or make promises and not keep them. You can also be just plain nasty by punishing your boyfriend with harsh consequences when you don't get what you want. The last way can be effective, but only with guys who don't know how needs are met respectfully.

If you're a girl who knows herself and respects others, you'll choose the first option. You'll see that the best way to get your needs met is simply to be honest. Explain to your boyfriend why the need is important to you — in other words, why it's reasonable that he should meet it. He may not want or be able to meet the need; after all, neither of you is going to say yes to every request to meet a need. Although you might feel hurt about not getting one of your favorite pet wants satisfied, you'll suck it up and try again later. That's the way life works.

your boyfriend's needs

Meeting your boyfriend's needs is a big part of adding to his happiness, but you have to be clear that you're meeting the needs of a Prince, not a Frog. Unfortunately, the way a guy gets his needs met from you often shows that he's truly a Frog. Respect and the rules of character apply to him just as they do to you.

When your boyfriend talks about negative feelings or unfulfilled needs, you might feel uncomfortable. Often guys aren't good at expressing themselves in relationships, and they can say upsetting things without intending to be disrespectful. For example, your boyfriend might tell you he didn't like something you supposedly said or did, and as a result he doesn't know if he wants to continue being your boyfriend. He may not actually want to break up with you. If what you did was disrespectful to him, he could simply be respecting himself and making clear how he wants you to treat him.

On the other hand, to give a big consequence to someone just because she refused to meet one of his needs — in other words, to punish that person — is nasty. Ethan asks Ella to be his idea of a sexy kitty and do things in bed that make her uncomfortable. She refuses. End of story? Not a chance — this is Ethan we're talking about here. He asks her to rethink her answer, telling her it'll be great, then hinting that if he can't get what he needs he's more than likely going to break up with her. She feels panicky, thinking, "Do I do this or not?"

Ella has to decide whether Ethan's pet want is reasonable. But that's not all. She also has to decide if she can satisfy Ethan's pet want and still respect herself. Ella should *first* decide whether Ethan's bedroom pet want links to her own genuine need. If she finds that doing what he wants doesn't connect to her desire need, then Ethan's pet want isn't reasonable. If she did it to please him, or to avoid losing him, she would have a hard time living with the consequences. When push comes to shove — and it often does in relationships — her beliefs, rules and needs come first. Period. Ella may have found herself face-to-face with a Frog who's being a bully with his bedroom pet want. It's far more important for Ella to decide what she wants than to worry about Ethan's threats to leave.

♡ HEART-SAVING SHORTCUT: Any guy who hints at a break-up based on your not satisfying one of his pet wants is using the threat to blackmail you into doing something you don't want to do. You'd be getting ripped off in this relationship because you deserve to have him shopping at your boutique for fulfillment of a gazillion needs, but all he's shopping for is a sexy kitty. It's you who should be telling him, "Mister, you have not considered my needs for one second, so I'm outta here!" And don't worry — you're still a sexy kitty, just not this Frog's!

Now let's look at how Frogs try to get their needs met. A tricky Frog might tell you he loves you, when he really doesn't, to get sex. A confused Frog might tell you he loves you (and really think he does) to get sex, then after getting the sex decide he didn't really love you after all. A nasty Frog might try to turn his problem into your problem by telling you that if you don't have sex with him, you're frigid. He might even say if you don't get over this problem, he'll leave.

The tricky guy is obviously disrespectful. Although he might not appear to be, the confused guy is too. He says "I love you" without thinking through what being in love really means. Worse, he doesn't understand himself well enough to know whether he's in love or not. The "I love you" line popped into his head, so he said it, at what he believed to be the right time. And the nasty guy is saying, "You can't be with me unless you behave the way I want you to."

In each of these three examples, the Frog is trying to get his needs met from you disrespectfully. The tricky Frog doesn't respect himself, or you, enough to tell the truth. The confused Frog doesn't respect himself enough to understand his own needs and feelings before professing love and asking you for sex. The nasty Frog doesn't respect himself at all. He thinks the only way he can get sex is to manipulate and threaten you. If *he* doesn't believe he's worth your time, why should you?

If you get your needs met from others by treating them with respect, you'll have great relationships in your life. You'll be a friend and a girlfriend who listens to others and who thinks things through before answering somebody's question. You'll be a person others can trust: what you say is honest and true, and what you commit to will be carried out.

All fairy tales have both Princes and Frogs, good and evil. To reach the lived-happily-ever-after part that's possible for each of us, we have to be able to spot Frogs. Frogs are not necessarily bad guys; they're just not the right guys for us. The trick is to recognize their Frog nature before we get hurt. Until you know who you are, you won't have good filtering skills; a guy's Frog warts will be invisible to you. Knock, knock. Who's there? A girl who has blind spots — Frog warts are invisible to her! Tricky Frogs don't say what they mean, confused Frogs don't follow through with what they say, and nasty Frogs don't know right from wrong so they use unsavory tactics to get their needs met from us.

Natalie now knows a little bit more about who she is as a person. Can you see any gaps in your own life between what you believe and what you do? Is there a gap between how you believe you should get your needs met and how you actually get them met? You can close these gaps with character. You'll truly respect yourself when you align your beliefs, feelings and needs with your To Do List.

Do you think that Ella and Ethan's love story will be different from Natalie and Ethan's? Ella now knows what she should be shopping for (list of needs to be met) in her relationship with Ethan. However, she doesn't yet have all the self-knowledge or tools she needs to figure out if Ethan is the right guy for her, let alone to build a relationship with any guy. She'll make better choices, yes. But she doesn't know how to get her needs met for herself or how she should let others get their needs met from her.

In the next chapter we'll look at how self-respect will help both Natalie and Ella take the next step onto the yellow-brick road.

THREE: *dating beliefs*

$\mathcal{Many}$ of us—perhaps most of us—don't respect ourselves and others. Nor do we expect others to respect us. Yet self-respect is the key to creating a beautiful life. It can do what strange coincidences do in childhood fairy tales: help us make speedy progress toward our own happy ending.

If we wrote a new kind of fairy tale about a woman who finds her Prince and lives (pretty much) happily ever after, what would that woman be like? She'd meet her needs using a To Do List and character, the building blocks of a beautiful life. She would not be like Cinderella, who had to wait for her fairy godmother to appear before she could get to the ball. Our Princess would definitely not be a damsel in distress, nor would she be chasing sexy bad-boy Frogs.

Our fairy-tale woman wouldn't play "He loves me, he loves me not," looking for signs of love in her little-picture Prince and Frog experiences. Instead, she'd make deliberate choices to meet her needs and those of her guy. If she wasn't able to have her needs met, or to meet her guy's needs, while still respecting herself and him, she'd strut to the exit singing "These Boots Were Made for Walking"—with attitude. Where does this attitude come from? It comes from knowing that you've made a tough self-respect choice. Sometimes, we feel the best about ourselves — respect ourselves the most — after making the hardest choices. You too can be one step closer to becoming this fairytale girl — once you nail this thing called self-respect!

Relationships with guys can be hard, partly because guys often don't ask but make rules for what they want. You might find that your boyfriend's rules have been made so that his unreasonable pet wants, not his needs, get satisfied. It's up to you to recognize what's going on and to show him that he must respect you. You have to use a "good-point stick" to get good at breaking your boyfriend's rules. What's a good-point stick?

A good-point stick is a concise, clear statement that communicates one person's beliefs or feelings about a certain issue to another person. In any conversation, these are points that make it possible for someone else to see your perspective. By contrast, going around and around in circles without being able to say what you mean doesn't make it easy for anybody to see your point of view. When you find yourself needing to clear something up between the two of you but you're missing great material, exit that conversation; come back to it when you have some good-point sticks. Strive to be a woman who doesn't retaliate with harsh words or threats when she gets hurt, but remains respectfully firm and uses specific points to explain her needs and how she expects to be treated.

In the following example, Natalie uses great material from her belief of respect to teach her new boyfriend Sean how to treat her. Sean gets frustrated when she's busy with her girlfriends and doesn't have time for him. He believes that if he's important to her, she should make him her number-one priority, putting him above even herself.

Natalie was at a dinner at Meghan's celebrating Gwen's recent promotion. She heard her phone but ignored it because she was listening to Gwen relate the conversation between her and her boss. Natalie's cell rang again. She picked it up.

NATALIE: What's up?

SEAN: You sound irritable — what's going on?

NATALIE: We're at dinner. What's up?

SEAN: I hate it when you get like this. You can't even take five minutes to talk to me?

NATALIE: I don't want to talk to you right now. I'll call you tomorrow. I need to get back to dinner…

SEAN: I want to talk now. Your girlfriends will understand that you have a boyfriend who wants to talk. By the way, why didn't you pick up the first time?

NATALIE: Sean, we were listening to Gwen's story.

SEAN: Treat me with some respect!

NATALIE: What?

SEAN: When I call, I want you to pick up the phone, no matter what!

NATALIE: That rule doesn't work for me. I'm not going to prove that you're important to me by not having fun with my girlfriends. Gotta go. Talk to you tomorrow.

What happens the next day will help Natalie determine what that little life-with-Frog experience means. Natalie used a good-point stick to stand up for herself — she refused to satisfy Sean's unreasonable pet want, which he mistakenly linked to his need to feel important.

If Sean were a Prince, he'd recognize and own up to his lack of respect; he'd take back his rule and be more considerate when Natalie was out with her girlfriends. A Prince looks for ways in which his girlfriend can meet his needs that include her feelings and needs too.

If Sean were a Frog, he'd stay angry at Natalie. He'll still expect her to satisfy his pet want to feel important, even when it means Natalie can't meet her own needs (to have fun with her girlfriends, for example). He'd be a controlling Frog if he insisted on getting his needs met by making rules to control

Natalie's actions. He'll continue to call her when he knows she's out with her girlfriends until she screams, "I give, I give! We'll do it your way!" That's life with a controlling Frog.

beliefs, rules and choices

We're born into a "me-me" world. As children, we instinctively put our own needs above those of others. We make choices based on what we feel we need at the moment. As small children — until about age three — we believe the world revolves around us, that everyone and everything exists to serve our needs. From a very early age, parents make our choices. Their rules meet their own needs — to keep us safe from harm and free from pain — so that our needs, to become the person we want to be and to grow happy, are also met.

As we grow up, the rules that come from family and social beliefs influence the choices we make. In some ways, social and dating choices are similar, but each brings its own set of beliefs, rules and consequences. Life is about choices and consequences: we learn lessons by experiencing how each choice makes us feel afterward. Whenever you break a family rule or one of society's laws, the consequence you experience is punishment, embarrassment, the hurt or disappointment you cause others, and so on. If you didn't like the experience, it makes sense that you wouldn't make that choice again. However, many people either ignore these experiences or never make the connection between their choices and the consequences.

Many people think that the bad consequences they suffer have little to do with their choices: "Whoever made the rules is out to get me," "Life is unfair," "Rules don't apply to me," "I just can't get a break," "The only mistake I made was getting caught." You've probably met people like that. They tend to repeat their choices and suffer the same lousy consequences over and over. Despite having all the information they've accumulated from their experiences, they don't use that information to make better choices. They just don't seem to get it. Do they not respect themselves enough to help themselves? Maybe, deep down, they don't believe they're worth it.

The consequences of not respecting yourself and others become more serious as you grow up. We're all faced with social choices, where choosing to break rules can lead to harsh consequences. If you choose to speed while driving, for instance, your experience might be a ticket or even a serious injury. If you choose to have unsafe sex, your experience might include an unplanned pregnancy or a sexually transmitted disease. If you choose to do drugs, like ecstasy or crystal meth, your experience might be addiction or death.

How do self-respect and choices relate to one another? The more you know and respect yourself, the better you'll become at making choices that lead to good experiences. When you make bad choices, as we all do, your self-respect will help you look back at what happened and make sense of it. Without enough self-respect to do this, people are more likely to find themselves living with bad choices and outcomes, as if they feel they don't deserve any better.

When you find yourself living with the consequences of a bad choice, think of your self-respect as a life jacket. Let your bad choice sink beneath the waves. Use your self-respect as a life jacket that lets you float safely away, catch your breath, and swim toward the land of your new choice, where you'll be safe. You're always worth it.

choices and consequences

There are choices you can make that cause ugly gossip, leaving you too embarrassed to get out of bed the next morning. Let's look at a scenario where Gwen, Ella's best friend, makes social choices and then experiences the consequences. They're on their way to a party at Sara's on Friday night. Gwen wants to enjoy herself and hang with her friends. When she gets to Sara's, she has a few drinks. By her fifth drink, she's flirting with Ella's Ethan…making out in the bathroom with Tim…putting on lip gloss — oops, she's dumped out her purse to find her gloss… there's her iPod on the floor…She winds up in a car with Tim, who's drunk-driving at NASCAR-type speeds!

The next day Gwen suffers a massive hangover, along with heaping spoonfuls of anxiety. Worse, she'll suffer the social consequences of her actions from the previous night. She's hurt Ella (broken the girl code) and herself (damaged her own reputation), and thanks to Sara's famous big mouth, everyone at the party will find out about the flirting and the bathroom make-out drama. She has no choice but to suck it up and call Ella to apologize, fully expecting that Ella will cool their friendship.

Any of us could have made Gwen's choices. She drank too much and broke a few of her own rules: not to flirt with her best friend's boyfriend, not to make out with guys she doesn't have feelings for and not to get into a car with a drunk driver. She started off with a simple need: to have fun building shared experiences with friends. She made choices that gave her immediate rewards at the party and on the way home, but she paid for the rewards in respect currency and she ended up feeling awful.

We all make good and bad choices. Our worst choices are sometimes made by default — by just letting things happen. It's always easier to just let life happen to us; it's much harder to make deliberate choices. If Gwen sees that last night's consequences happened because of how many drinks she chose to have — not because "Life is unfair"— then the next time she goes to a party she might follow a two- or three-drink rule. If she follows this rule, she can still have fun but isn't as likely to break her other rules while she does. She'll make sure she's still able to include her beliefs and the feelings of others in her choices.

If you find yourself living with the consequences of a bad choice, you need to reconnect with your self-respect. When you've made an honest mistake, grab a life jacket: forgive yourself, keep on practising character and make a different choice the next time. When you make honest mistakes, the learning loop works like a Get Out of Jail Free card in Monopoly — it gets you back into the game. But when you repeatedly make the same bad choices, it's more difficult for you and others to shrug and chalk them up to lessons learned. To make the best choices, we must look at the bigger picture, which includes our beliefs and our understanding of our needs and the feelings and needs of others.

Let's see how Ella can use the learning loop to take back control of her life. With misgivings, she agreed to do what Ethan wanted in bed. Afterward, she felt something wasn't right between her and Ethan. At Sara's party, Ethan was flirting with not only Gwen (her best friend) but with Sara and others as well. She tried talking to Ethan about it the next morning but got nowhere fast. She feels different with Ethan now, and maybe he feels different too — she's not sure. But the relationship doesn't feel right.

Ella needs to look at the bigger picture, which includes her beliefs, her understanding of her needs and her feelings about whether or not Ethan is the right guy for her. She needs to talk to him about her confused feelings to find a way to become clear and not confused about her relationship. Or maybe she needs to make an exit choice. If she can't make these types of deliberate choices, she'll likely find herself staying with Ethan because she doesn't respect herself enough to leave. And when we don't respect ourselves enough to figure out what our consequences mean, and to act on them, it's easy to convince ourselves that we don't deserve better.

familiar dating beliefs

Beliefs for how to build a shared relationship that is respectful and wonderful come from many sources: from your experiences with guys, from observing the experiences of your girlfriends or parents, and from TV shows, movies and magazines. We create rules from our beliefs. For instance, from your beliefs you might make this rule for yourself: not to kiss or have sex on a first date. Or you might have other rules for dating, based on familiar dating beliefs, like "Follow your heart," "Love is enough," "All's fair in love and war," "Relationships take work," "Accept a guy for who he is, warts and all" and "We're here for a good time, not a long time." (I swear a Frog made that one up.)

Let's say you actually believe that all's fair in love and war. What rules would you include in your dating choices? Actually, all the character rules for how you or your boyfriend should get your needs met by one another would fly out the window. What rules would inform your choices if you believed you should follow your heart? Well, you'd make choices — heart-over-head choices — that didn't include your beliefs, in order to keep your boyfriend happy at any price — bypassing any rules you might have.

We all have different rules for how our boyfriends should treat us and what needs we deserve to get met from them. These rules often grow out of beliefs that don't help us respect ourselves — or our boyfriend. If we simply accept life-with-a-Frog experiences, we're teaching that boyfriend that it's okay to behave like a Frog. To avoid becoming lost, we have to adopt new beliefs, like a belief in character, for how we get our needs met and how our boyfriends should treat us.

Relationships are like a maze. Most of us follow our heart, doing the best we can to use the beliefs that are familiar to us to make and check our choices. Each new choice takes us further into the relationship maze. Our choices can either keep us on the right path to the exit or leave us hopelessly lost.

risk vs. reward

Often in relationships we look only at the little picture and make risk/reward choices that seem right in the moment. We assess the risk and then make the best choice we can to get the immediate reward we're seeking. Remember Natalie and her new boyfriend, Sean? What if he threatened to break up with her if she didn't promise to answer all his calls, period? And suppose she'd agreed, to avoid a break-up. She would have been making a risk/reward choice. The immediate rewards would have been Sean's short-term happiness — no argument, no break-up. He'd say "Love ya" and let her get back to her girlfriends.

There are problems with such risk/reward choices. First, the reward is almost always temporary. Now that he knows Natalie will give in, Sean will be back with more dreadful demands — backed up with harsh threats. Second, when we satisfy a pet want while not respecting ourselves, we pay dearly for these choices. Although she might not have realized it, Natalie would have paid a high price for giving in to Sean to keep him happy. After the good feelings wore off, she'd feel anxious and maybe even a little sick. And third, these choices almost always lead to rerun arguments. Sooner or later, Natalie would get careless about answering Sean's calls and he'd start the argument and the threats all over again, reminding her of her promise.

Finally, risk/reward decisions can be addictive. When we make such decisions to keep our boyfriends happy, which we often do in the heat of the moment, we remember the good feeling of the reward, not the sick, let-down feeling that later tells us the decision was wrong. These risk/reward decisions take us deeper into the maze until we become lost.

The first step toward understanding why some consequences hurt and some feel blissful is recognizing the connection between the choice that led to the experience of that consequence. Deliberately looking for this connection is the key to making better choices; the awareness that results will help you get to know yourself better. Of course, you're still going to make choices you'll wish you hadn't made. But making sense of your choices — good and bad — will give you a better chance of making the right choice the next time. This is how you build a collection of positive experiences, and how you increase self-respect. Your reward: a more carefree kind of life, with less struggling.

Unlike risk/reward choices, choices made using the learning loop (needs-choices-consequences) take the big picture of your beautiful life into account. These choices will include your beliefs, feelings and needs. The choices you make using the learning loop will become steps in a lifelong process of building self-knowledge and a sense of value.

In the framework of the learning loop, there are five steps that will ultimately become second nature to you:

- Understanding yourself and your needs
- Making choices based on that understanding
- Evaluating the consequences of your choices (observing what happens when you make them)
- Taking direct action — making a new choice if you need to (because the first one didn't work out as you thought it would)
- Adjusting your self-knowledge and needs (as you did with the pink top experience)

Below is a set of dating beliefs that will help you understand yourself and your needs in a relationship. They'll assist you in making and checking your choices, always keeping the idea of respect in mind. The objective of these dating beliefs is to help you exit the maze — either hand-in-hand with your Prince or alone, having decided to send your Frog back to the pond. Either choice is one you should feel proud of.

dating beliefs

Here are four dating beliefs that will help you get to the fairy tale that is possible. For any relationship to work, you must believe that:

- He is the draw for me
- I like myself when I'm with him
- I like him as a person independent of me
- I am the draw for him

Just as schools create rules to ensure that the needs of every student — to learn and grow, to be challenged and supported — are met, you can use these dating beliefs to make your own rules to ensure your needs — to love and be loved, to learn and grow in a compatible relationship — can be met.

The list of the needs we have doesn't magically arrive on our Sweet 16th birthday. We search for what we need in order to be happy, yes, without really knowing what we're looking for and with few clues to help us recognize the need when we experience it.

In *The Wizard of Oz* there are four main characters: Dorothy, the Tin Man, the Lion and the Scarecrow. Each is shopping for fulfillment. On their journey they are searching for ways to get their needs met. Dorothy is shopping for a way to get back home to Kansas, the Tin Man is looking for a heart, the Lion needs courage and the Scarecrow requires a brain.

These characters go on a journey to do the Wizard's dirty work in order to get a reward (their needs met). Alas, the

Wizard is not only a big talker but a fake. Don't despair, however, because the characters end up with what they each need. You see, those characters had what they thought was missing all along; they just didn't recognize they did, not even while they were experiencing that very specific need getting met on their journey.

Let's use the Scarecrow's experience to understand ourselves a little better. Like the others, the Scarecrow wanted the Wizard to meet a need he had in fact already met for himself. The Wizard awarded him an honorary degree, based on the Scarecrow's track record during the journey — getting the group out of tight spots. Since we don't want to be like the Scarecrow, we can take this away from his journey: believe you have value so you don't expect to be validated, that is to look for others to confirm your value.

Second, we *do* want to be like Dorothy. She acquired self-knowledge on her yellow-brick road; to get back to her life all she had to do was click her heels three times and wake up. The information contained in the dating beliefs describes how other girls have experienced getting their own needs met. So each of the dating beliefs contains a list of needs, along with some clues, to help you understand when you are experiencing a met or unmet need. Knowing better means doing better. When you know what your needs are, you will deliberately look for when any one of these needs is getting met or not. And like Dorothy, you'll click your own heels three times and wake up!

Up to this point, we've talked about the needs that you are responsible for meeting yourself and the needs you should expect others, including your boyfriend, to meet. I am now going to regroup these same needs into the four dating beliefs so that with practice you will be able to make choices in your own relationship that include your beliefs, feelings and needs.

is he the draw for me?

You must understand what this belief means before you use it to inform your choices. The word "draw" basically means "one who attracts and holds interest," but my use of the word here is broader than that. If your boyfriend is the draw for you, you feel compelled to meet his needs. Why? Because doing so brings you pleasure, not because you feel you should meet them or because you want something in return. You strive to meet his needs because you're hungry for the feeling you get in that moment when you meet them. If your boyfriend is the draw for you, his happiness can sometimes mean as much to you as your own — or even more. You know the saying "It's better to give than to receive"? Have you ever given someone a present that brings tears of joy to his or her eyes? How did it make you feel? That's exactly the feeling you get when you're drawn to meet your boyfriend's needs, simply because you know how happy it will make him.

Now to that sweet little thing called chemistry, or "love at first sight." Chemistry draws you to your yummy new boyfriend. It also keeps you interested. While wickedly delightful, chemistry is *not* love and the presence of chemistry does not mean that a guy will still be the draw for you once the effects of chemistry have worn off.

How does chemistry work? If you've ever had a serious case of love at first sight, you know: your palms sweat, you're afraid to look into the guy's eyes (but you do) and everything you say sounds silly or seems to come out wrong. When you do connect with him, you become driven to be with him; when you can't be with him, you ache for the nearness of him. So why is chemistry wicked? Because it's a double-edged sword. When chemistry is working, it may be possible to get your need to love met three ways: loving yourself, loving him and being loved. But chemistry is just as likely to lead to a nightmare story — being with a guy who attracts and then holds your interest not because all your needs are being met but because you've become a slave to your chemistry-met need. Natalie felt physical chemistry with Ethan, and she confused it with love.

Why do we feel chemistry with one guy and not another? It's a mystery. A compatible relationship experience is about groups of needs getting meet: emotional, physical, intellectual and lifestyle. Chemistry, on the other hand, is often about just one need being fulfilled. Perhaps chemistry happens when someone meets one of our needs for the first time, when we feel a need getting really — *really* — met or when someone meets one of the needs we're not able to meet ourselves. So when you feel chemistry — when your palms get sweaty, your heart races and you're light-headed — simply try to figure out which need is being met.

Why? When chemistry is attached to any one of your needs being met by your boyfriend, you develop feelings of love. When this happens you'll start to grow happy and, like magic, you'll feel as if *all* of your needs are being met. Welcome to the illusion of love.

When you feel chemistry with someone, think of it as nature's way of saying, "Pay attention! This person brings something either really wonderful or really horrible to the next part of your life." Pay attention to what? To the consequences! Chemistry leads to actions, which lead to consequences. If the consequences leave you feeling happy, respected and healthy — if you can look at yourself in the mirror and see yourself growing happy — then your chemistry might turn into real love. If, instead, the consequences leave you feeling guilty, hurt, frightened or confused — perhaps unable to look in the mirror at all — then the chemistry you feel is probably a danger sign.

If you have chemistry with your guy, it does not mean he's the draw for you. It means you have chemistry. You should only believe your boyfriend is the draw for you if you keep experiencing your needs being met. In other words, you don't notice that any one of your needs is frequently going unmet.

If your guy is the draw for you, you will find yourself wanting to introduce him to your friends and family, to help him with his To Do List and to start paying attention to his feelings. Before you even know what his motives are you'll find yourself taking on a forgiving heart — excusing his actions, believing everything he says and showing him that you value him by talking to him about your feelings.

If you believe your guy is the draw for you, you'll be able to see how attractive he is even if no other girl on the planet can. For starters, you'll notice things about him that your single girlfriends shouldn't, like how you can see his chest muscles move under the fabric whenever he wears that white T-shirt. (Of course, that T-shirt's your favorite.) You'll desire attention and affection from him so much you'll probably be drawn into deploying "girly-girl" strategies. One of these is playing hard-to-get, which increases the risk of ramping up the "fog index" for any guy. You may, for example, go beyond the usual intelligence gathering and try to find out where he's going to be at a certain time so that "by chance" you can show up. You discover he's going to be at a party at so-and-so's house, so you get there, put on extra makeup, roll your skirt up at the waist and ignore him while you hang out in a corner flirting with his friends. This is playing hard-to-get.

While we feel compelled to get noticed, what can start out as a great idea designed to attract can actually undermine your plan to draw the guy in. For example, your girly-girl tactics worked: you and the guy are having a conversation and you're feeling as if you just got a juicy pet want satisfied. Yet your plan is to cut the encounter short, so you're looking for the perfect moment to end it. Why? You want to draw him back to you, tease him, kind of like a movie trailer, so he'll seek you out for another conversation. The high fog index for the guy — the reason he ends up really confused — comes from the fact that your actions don't show him whether you are interested in him or not. You desire attention and affection from him. This desire will grow as you spend more time with him, eventually turning you into your own version of sexy kitty.

In order to believe that your boyfriend is the draw for you, you must be able to meet your need to be clear and not confused as to whether or not you and he share enough beliefs and goals to make the relationship compatible. You both will have certain beliefs about how the world works, from politics to religion, about how relationships work and about the difference between right and wrong. From your beliefs, each one of you will build rules, form opinions and have judgements about people, situations and events. If he is the draw for you, you must be able to continue to listen to your thinking voice and to challenge his beliefs if they're different from your own, thus meeting your own need to be clear and not confused. Without beliefs similar to yours, your boyfriend won't hold your interest; you'll be drawn away from him, not toward him.

You and he might have different morals, come from different cultures or have different religious practices. If so, you'll have to respectfully challenge your boyfriend, listen to him and understand how these different beliefs might affect his choices. Self-respect and respect for others are principles that cross all cultures. For your relationship to work and be fun, you must be open-minded and supportive of your boyfriend's choices. This is easier said than done, however, because we all make judgements about how others act and what they say. Others will judge your choice in boyfriends the same way they judge what you wear. So if your boyfriend doesn't share the same self-respect belief as you, if he makes choices to behave disrespectfully at parties and say disrespectful things in front of your friends or co-workers, they'll judge him. And so should you!

To meet your intellectual need to understand—to feel clear and not confused—you must be confident that both you and your guy have the same idea about where your relationship is going. You should discuss what your big-picture expectations and beliefs and rules are for *any* relationship. You should both talk generally about what you're looking for. For example, are you a high-touch person (who loves to hold hands and be hugged) or a low-touch person? If you're high-touch, you should shop for a high-touch boyfriend. Otherwise, you won't get your desire need met. Do you want the relationship to be open or not? (In a relationship that's not open, you both agree not to date other people). You'll either share similar dating expectations or you won't. Don't be afraid to tell a guy what your expectations really are or what type of relationship you're looking for. Don't feel embarrassed by what you want or expect. If it's not what he wants, he'll tell you (if you're listening). Isn't it much better to know now rather than later when you see his real intentions in his actions, like him arriving at a movie with another girl?

You will experience getting your need to be clear and not confused about your relationship met when you know where you stand: are you his girlfriend or not? Ask questions to close the gap between what you and he are shopping for: "What are we doing here? Are we going out? Do you go out with other girls besides me?" Which question should you ask first? The one you're most scared to ask. And be brave in the face of the possible kiss-of-death rejection — the consequence being this is not love — if he says you're just friends. This guy has just revealed to you that his real expectation for this relationship is "friends with benefits." Does that work for you? If so, great. If not, you've just saved yourself a lot of heartache.

For you and your boyfriend to build a compatible relationship, your goals have to be similar — not only for where you want your relationship to go, but for your own beautiful lives too. Most often, the deal breaker in a relationship comes when you don't agree on which needs are important to be met in your own beautiful lives. Naturally, it's hard to support choices we don't agree with. If you and your boyfriend valued different levels of luxury, you would prioritize your lifestyle needs differently. For example, your differing pet wants would probably be the deal breaker if your boyfriend wanted to live in a mansion and you'd be content to live in a trailer. You'd have different To Do Lists. Your boyfriend would have a very busy To Do List, perhaps sacrificing fulfillment of many of his needs while he built the lifestyle he wanted. You would likely never compromise your physical, intellectual or emotional needs without a fight. It would be difficult to figure out a shared To Do List that would allow each of you to grow happy in this relationship. You might feel chemistry for this guy, but he'd more than likely end up not being enough of a draw for you and the relationship probably wouldn't work.

If your boyfriend is the draw for you, you'll feel alive with him. You'll take extra time to get ready and make extra time for him because he's important to you. You'll do things he likes to do or you'll be helpful with his To Do List. And of course you'll do special things for him (to please him even more). You'll be excited to spend time with him and it will be hard to wait for the next time you go out together. You'll protect him fiercely, keeping him safe from those who criticize him even if their criticism has merit or truth — we shouldn't do this, but we do.

do i like myself when i'm with him?

Remember when Meghan told Natalie how different she was since she'd been going out with Ethan? You might think that some guys have a knack for being able to change a girl's traits.

But in reality your boyfriend can only change your traits when you stop building self-knowledge. If you continue to meet your needs, on the other hand, you'll have lots of "pink top" experiences, when you become more familiar with yourself. Changing your traits, what you like to do or who you want to become, is acceptable as long as *you're* making deliberate choices to do so.

If you keep meeting your need to value yourself, you'll say what you think and act like the person you know yourself to be — except that when you're with your boyfriend you'll have better material: you'll be extra funny, flirty and witty. And the best of your traits will shine: you'll be kinder, more generous, more thoughtful, more attentive. Stay important to yourself — make sure you're taking care of yourself first and making good choices, just as you did before you met this yummy creature. For example, you'll continue to meet your need to be safe by showing up for work (if you have a job) and by making great choices (like not spending your rent money on new outfits to please him), thus ensuring that you have food and shelter. You'll be meeting your need to value others by staying connected to the other people — friends and family — in your life. Continuing to meet these needs keeps you stay confident, productive and in control of your life.

do i like him as a person independent of me?

To love anyone you must get to know that person; otherwise, what you actually love is your illusion of that person, not who he really is. The confusing part about Princes and Frogs is that they often act the same in the beginning. So don't get disappointed in your judgement if the guy you thought was Mr. Perfect starts showing himself to be not so perfect after all. At the same time, don't keep hoping that the great guy in him is going to magically reappear. You know how you try to make a good impression when you first meet people? How agreeable you are? How willing to do things to make others happy? And how you start relaxing and revealing more of yourself as you get to know them better, and then start to expect — even demand — that your own needs get met? Guess what: guys do that too!

So in exactly the same way that you work at becoming familiar with yourself, you do that with him. Just as you see not only the best in yourself but your shortcomings as well, you do that with him. This is how you determine if your traits and his blend beautifully like warm apple pie and ice cream. It's also how you know when they clash like dark chocolate and asparagus. For example, you might be easygoing while he's moody and controlling; it's easy to see that these two traits won't mix well. Getting to know him includes understanding when he gives you that nod or certain facial expression at a party that tells you it's time to leave or that you might want to rethink what you're telling others in a social conversation. It also means getting to know as many of his favorite things as possible, like food, sports, movies and books.

You can't accept your boyfriend just because you really like him. You must build a clear picture of his Frog warts. And don't think he doesn't have any; we all do. Does he listen to your point of view? How does he act when it's *difficult* for you to meet his needs (for example, when he really wants something and you don't want to give it to him)? Watch how he treats other people and who he has chosen as friends. Observe how his friends and family act toward him and note what they say about him. You're looking to see if he knows himself and what his own needs are. You're looking for a guy you don't feel you must control; he is capable and in control of his own To Do List. Judge the choices he makes to determine how well he knows and values himself and others. The way he meets his own needs and closes the gaps in his own To Do List will tell you if your boyfriend is capable, confident and in control of his life.

♡ HEART-SAVING SHORTCUT: The choices your boyfriend makes in his lifestyle area will tell you whether your beliefs are similar or not. If you see him making choices to take care of himself first and build himself a beautiful life, and respecting himself and others, it's likely that your beliefs are similar enough for a compatible relationship.

am i the draw for him?

For you to be able to believe that you are the draw for him, your boyfriend must be compelled to meet each of his needs at your boutique; otherwise, the needs you deserve to have fulfilled won't get met. If you're the draw for him, you'll encounter signposts that indicate he is moving deeper into the relationship. The first signpost is when he includes you in the other relationships in his life — with his best friend and family members, for example. His willingness to bring you into his innermost circle speaks to his intent for a relationship with you. He won't introduce you into his other significant relationships until he's sure he'll be seeing you regularly. When a guy tells other people in his life that you're important to him and he expects them to treat you well, you've passed this signpost. You'll know he's told them that you're important to him because they'll be nice to you and treat you with respect in order to please him, whether they know you or not. At this stage, you'll also be bringing him into your relationships with friends and family.

The second signpost appears when you begin to help each other with your To Do Lists. It's one thing to support your boyfriend's activities, especially when it takes time away from you; it's quite another to take the time to physically do things to help him in his life. We each have only so many minutes to get what we need done each day. When you choose to invest time in someone else's To Do List, you know he's important to you. What do friends do? They help each other. In any relationship, each of us must be willing to help the other.

In any caring relationship, you must balance your To Do List and his. This balance becomes a shared To Do List. What goes on this list is the result of respectful communication and negotiation, and of a willingness to meet each other's needs to be helped and pleased and to feel important. It can be a delicate balance. If you go to his game on Saturday night, he should happily go to your sister's piano recital on Sunday afternoon. If he helps you prepare for your parents' surprise anniversary party, you should be willing to help him clean out his grandparents' garage. If your To Do List is not very full and you want a boyfriend to get busy with a shared To Do List (even though his own list is already chock-full), there may be conflicts about how much time either of you is willing to invest in this relationship. On the other hand, if he's asking you to cut and paste onto your To Do List stuff his mother used to do for him, you can politely tell him to wash his own clothes, make his own lunches and clean his own room.

The third signpost is cleared when your boyfriend begins to pay serious attention to your feelings, as if he can sense whether you're feeling good or bad without your having to tell him. When you do tell him, he'll respond as if you're the only person in the world at that moment. He's honest with you and tells you how he feels, and he's clear about whether or not he feels the same way you do. His willingness to be emotionally available tells you a great deal about whether or not he knows himself and what he wants to meet his needs.

Until your relationship moves through this invisible timeline, think of your yummy creature not as a boyfriend but as a *new* boyfriend. The difference between a guy you just started to see and a real boyfriend is similar to the difference between a girlfriend and a best friend. You spend more time with your best friend than you do with a girlfriend. You share your feelings with her more deeply than with a new girlfriend. You're more willing to make sacrifices for your best friend to meet her needs than you are for other girlfriends. When we forget that there's a huge difference between a new boyfriend and a boyfriend, we can misread our boyfriend's actions when we try to answer the daisy question — and get hurt as a result. If you've been seeing a guy for months yet you haven't moved past these three signposts, your boyfriend is still a new boyfriend and you won't have a clue whether you're the draw for him or not.

As your boyfriend moves through his timeline, you should begin to feel more of your needs being met in each of your needs areas. As this happens you'll grow to believe you are the draw for him. If you're the draw for him, he'll be curious about you. He'll try to become familiar with who you are and how to meet your needs. He'll accept you for who you are and forgive you for any honest mistakes you make. We all make honest mistakes in relationships; on occasion, we make really stupid mistakes. Nobody's perfect. Some of our mistakes can be fixed with a conversation and a "Sorry." Others simply can't be fixed — only forgiven, which is okay. You'll know that your mistakes have been truly forgiven when your boyfriend doesn't bring them up in an argument about something else.

You'll know he finds you attractive because he tells you. If he asks to see you again or kisses you, he likes you. Shortly after that first lovely kiss, you begin to feel his desire for physical affection. But don't believe that his moving to the make-out stage is always a reliable indication of true affection.

At some point you begin to recognize your boyfriend's feelings of love for you, and your need to be loved is met. You feel you're meeting his needs and satisfying his pet wants. You feel valued because you have great conversations where he talks to you about what he thinks and feels — he's emotionally available to you. You notice a wonderful change when he talks to you: you feel more tenderness in his voice.

When you're the draw for your boyfriend, he's interested in you and you feel this interest when he asks you about yourself. In conversations about your beliefs and opinions, he supports or sometimes challenges you. Regardless, he accepts and understands you, so you feel he's listening. Notice if he acts like this when you're with friends as well as in private.

If you're the draw for your boyfriend, he'll have energy to do things with you. When you're together, he'll act as if he really wants to be with you. He'll treat you differently from others by putting your feelings and needs above theirs. In his choices he'll include what you like to do and takes your feelings into account. As long as you see him making time for things you enjoy doing or have to get done, he's meeting your need to feel important and helped. He calls you, and he pays attention to you when you're out with friends. He takes care of your needs and your safety just as he takes care of his own. If you're going skiing and the weather is extra cold, he'll remind you to grab warmer clothes. When you go out with him, you feel protected and safe.

The dating beliefs will give you great information to determine whether your boyfriend measures up to your standards for respectful behavior. You'll find that by using the dating beliefs in the same way you use your family and social beliefs — to make and check your choices — your experiences will be more wonderful with your boyfriend. If you don't, it'll be hard to manage your hurt feelings in any shared experience with him. If from the get-go you want to choose a yummy boyfriend you'll build yourself a great bar. Then again, if you're already in a relationship and you build yourself a great bar, bonus. You'll see what your girlfriends see: your boyfriend as he really is, Frog warts and all.

How do you build yourself a bar? In the next chapter you'll find out.

FOUR: *setting your bar*

Natalie now has a better understanding of who she is than she did when she was with Ethan. She's started to treat herself — and others — with more respect. Getting here has involved a great deal of personal development. Will all this work be enough to build herself a beautiful life? No, but it's a start. Knowing and respecting yourself and others is important, but it's a only part of the big picture. To build a beautiful life, you have to make others aware of when they're not treating you with respect — then insist that they do. Natalie started to do this when she refused to make Sean her number-one priority by putting him above even herself. She got off the phone and back to her girlfriends.

Ever had a friend who talks behind your back, tells your secrets? We get hurt and upset by this treatment, and may even protest weakly, but we don't really do anything about it. Natalie herself chose to do nothing when Elizabeth spilled her guts to Tim — she avoided the hard conversation. Would you? Have you ever said, "Why are you telling my secrets and making up stories about me? I want you to stop." Or, "I don't get it. I thought we were friends, yet you're not thinking about my feelings, and you're not respecting me when you say this stuff about me." No matter how much you talk about who you are, people know you by what you do. It's up to each of us to respect ourselves and others, and to expect others to respect us, both in how they treat us and how they choose to get their needs met from us.

♡ HEART-SAVING SHORTCUT: Life is a mirror. Ever had a friend who puts you down, or talks behind your back, making fun of you? How each of your friends treats you is a reflection of yourself. It tells you something about what you believe about yourself and what you show others you deserve. Life has a way of bringing us exactly what we believe we deserve. Or, more accurately, we let people into our lives and create situations for ourselves that reflect what down deep we think we are worth.

Ever had a friend who really knows how to respect herself? If you've ever told a girlfriend's secret to another, been caught and then asked to stop talking to others about what she tells you, you have such a self-respecting friend. When we don't expect to be valued, we make choices that harm our self-worth. Your girlfriend wouldn't make such choices — she values herself. Your learning loop: you've experienced a girlfriend who not only knows how to respect herself but also tries to get you to treat her more respectfully. Perfect. Copycat that girl!

Your bar is the standard for how you should treat yourself and others, and for how you expect to be treated. The height of your bar isn't marked in feet, inches or centimeters. How high it is depends on how you expect to be treated in your relationship. If you value yourself, then only *some* guys will treat you with enough respect to clear your bar. If your bar is too low, just about anyone can jump over it and into your life, whether they treat you respectfully or not.

You need to know what's possible in a relationship so that you don't settle for life with a Frog. At the start of any relationship, we don't have much more than our feelings to help us see whether we're with a Prince or a Frog. It's a time when many women believe "Yes, yes, yes! My boyfriend is the draw for me" and fall head over heels in love (even though it's not the first time they've fallen in love that year). This is probably not love. It's more likely the *illusion* of love, which gets built from all those early conversations, kisses and intimate experiences with your boyfriend that make you smile and laugh afterward. *Real* love is what you experience in the middle of the relationship, when your boyfriend is happily meeting your needs (and maybe some you didn't even know you had!) and you're happily meeting his, all the while maintaining your self-respect and working on your To Do List.

You can only set your bar according to what you know. Maybe you've never experienced a compatible relationship. Maybe you've only gone out with guys who didn't respect your feelings or didn't want to get to know you as a person. Maybe you weren't fortunate enough to watch your parents in a loving relationship, and so you have a bar that accepts constant fighting and disrespect. Maybe you watched your mom meet your dad's needs while not expecting to get her needs met in return. In that case you might have a bar that doesn't expect fulfillment of all those beautiful needs you deserve to have met too. On the other hand, if your bar is based on romantic movies, only Prince Charming himself could reach it, and that guy doesn't exist.

After you've chosen a boyfriend, your bar will help you figure out if your needs are getting met and help you see the difference between a genuine need and a pet want. Your bar will help you figure out if you're maintaining your self-respect while meeting your boyfriend's needs. It will also help you know if your boyfriend is being respectful while getting his needs met from you. Your bar will always help you close the gap between what you're experiencing and what you deserve.

your hurt list

At some point in any relationship, you'll have confused, mixed or hurt feelings and you'll struggle over whether to stay with your boyfriend or leave. If you repeatedly experience disappointment, you're probably not getting what you need in the relationship. Hurt feelings are like warning signals that tell you your boyfriend probably isn't able to treat you with enough respect to clear your bar. These little alarm bells tell you to pay attention: you're experiencing unmet needs in the relationship.

Sometimes feeling hurt is a minor thing; at other times it means you should run from the relationship as fast as you can. When you feel hurt or confused, write down either the words your boyfriend said or the things he did that caused you to feel that way. This is your Hurt List. Writing down what he said or did — or both — and how this made you feel is the way you begin to meet your own need to be clear and not confused.

To get out of being lost in love, you have to figure out what the items in your Hurt List mean — how they link to your needs. To judge a situation clearly, you must be able to make sense of your feelings. However, you must have great information in order to judge a situation; you get this information from the dating beliefs.

Your Hurt List items can either be about you or they could have everything to do with your boyfriend. It can be hard sometimes to decide whose need isn't getting met because there are two different sets of needs in a relationship: yours and his! When shouldn't an item be on your Hurt List? Say your boyfriend's been really busy, working toward some short-term deadline or life goal (a big exam, a promotion). There you sit with an empty shared To Do List. You feel ignored, a little hurt, not as pleased or important as you did. Yet before this happened, in the big picture, you were the draw for one another and growing happy.

Since it's impossible to leave hurt feelings in a relationship for too long without disconnecting, you're going to be compelled to do something about your feelings. Let's use a "needs question" to set your bar for how you expect to get your need to feel important met. A needs question is like a good-point stick you use during a conversation — it helps you to see a situation not only from your point of view but from someone else's.

When you see a situation clearly you can usually avoid big gaps between what you believe and how you act. Remember the dating beliefs? "Each one of you must be able to help or support the other with his or her To Do List." If you believed that, you'd expect to be helped and supported and vice versa. Yet if you didn't help or support your boyfriend, you'd ignore your own rules and you'd create a gap between what you believe and what you do. Using your bar helps you eliminate gaps. When you use it, you'll find fewer instances of not respecting yourself or others.

In the scenario above, ask yourself: am I supporting my boyfriend with his To Do List? If your answer is no, you're living in your me-me world, getting ready to nag your boyfriend while he's trying to build himself a beautiful life. You're trumping your boyfriend's *experience* — his trying to meet his need to be safe — with your need to be important. See how the needs question helped you to understand your hurt feelings better?

If you didn't have a bar, you could easily have chosen to demand (rather than ask) that he spend time with you *now*, regardless of his needs. But you'd be asking him to give up his self-respect. Instead, you could say to yourself: "Suck it up, buttercup. He has a really good reason for not spending time with me." Make a choice that includes his feelings and needs: drop him off some cupcakes, tell him how you feel and ask when you can expect to see more of him.

Sometimes, though, the items on your Hurt List can have everything to do with your boyfriend. They might have shown up often enough on your Hurt List to become a pattern. Let's call these "red flags." Here's how a Hurt List item becomes a red flag. You notice your boyfriend has gone out with his friends three times in a row without including you. More Hurt List items show up: he calls less often, he's busier than usual. You now see a pattern in your list: your boyfriend is investing less time in meeting your needs. You don't feel as loved as you did before. What to do? Tell him you feel you're no longer the draw for him. The guy will more than likely tell you he loves you, and immediately include you more fully in his plans —"On Monday, let's go hear some music."

After that kind of discussion, it's hard to manage your feelings of worry and anxiety. (He doesn't love me as much as he used to!) You must wait for his actions, to see if he follows through. This is hard: it's like writing a tough exam and then having to wait to see whether you passed. But part of managing your feelings is giving your boyfriend enough time to make sense of his and then respond to your concerns. A Prince gets back to you with reassuring words, perhaps an apology, and changes his actions. He's simply gotten lost in his priorities, as we all do sometimes. After the discussion he begins making choices to spend more time with you — to please you — doing stuff you both enjoy.

Now let's look at the same experience with a Frog. You flag your repeated Hurt List items and discuss them. Your boyfriend tells you he's totally into the relationship, he loves you and he changes his actions right away. This "new man" stays around for about a week, then goes right back to excluding you from his plans. His behavior confirms that you have an unmet need, so you can expect this argument to appear in your relationship again. Now, if you believe that you know and like yourself (you're building a beautiful life), you can be sure this isn't about you; it's about your boyfriend.

To build a relationship, you have to manage your Hurt List. You make sense of your feelings by understanding which of you is responsible for them. Once you've set your bar, your boyfriend will have to clear the bar — meet your needs — for you to let him into your life in a more serious way.

What happens when he tries to clear your bar, but you don't think he jumped high enough? Do you suck it up and accept him as a Prince who meets most of your needs, or do you complain that he didn't meet them in exactly the way you thought he should? Remember, your Hurt List items can easily be about your own unreasonable expectations. So ask yourself, "Am I upset just because he didn't jump over my bar exactly as I pictured he would — frontward, backward, with a smile on his face?" If so, that's okay, but make sure you're behaving like a fair, regal woman — not a selfish, stuck-up one who doesn't respect herself or others.

Elizabeth expects Jordan — if he really loves her — to treat Valentine's Day as a major occasion, like Christmas, with treats and trimmings. And say Jordan's driven to meet her needs, to the point of rescuing her from flat tires and taping her favorite shows without her even asking. She's enjoying Valentine's Day: she's opened her presents, and she's waiting to find out where he's taking her for dinner. Oops — surprise! Elizabeth's not going out for dinner. Jordan's made it himself. There she sits, pouting, with an unsatisfied pet want — dinner in a nice restaurant.

Some women would die to have their guy make them a nice dinner — or at least try. There's a bit of Princess in all of us; we can be self-absorbed like Elizabeth, who did not recognize that he made that dinner because he loved her. That's called acting entitled, as if it's our God-given right to get that pet want satisfied exactly as we dreamed it would be. It's great that Elizabeth is able to tell Jordan how she expects a need to be met, but it's up to him to decide how he wants to meet it. And if her only argument is that she's a Princess, she should be prepared to downsize her throne to at least a nice cozy armchair.

Often, hurt, mixed or disappointed feelings result from reasonable pet wants going unsatisfied. The price you pay for ignoring these items on your Hurt List is reduced self-worth, whether the items are about you or about your boyfriend. Let's look at how Hurt List items link to unmet needs.

he is the draw for me

What Hurt List items (hurt, mixed or confused feelings) might you experience when you believe your boyfriend's the draw for you, but he isn't? You'll find yourself no longer interested in getting your needs met at his boutique — even losing interest in getting needs met that you were once driven to meet. For example, your intellectual need to be interested might erode to where you can't wait for your boyfriend to finish talking so you can get off the phone. If you find yourself noticing other guys or becoming really attracted to another guy, your boyfriend is likely not the draw for you.

Each of us needs a sense of where our relationship is going. You must have the same expectation as your boyfriend; you must be moving in the same direction through your invisible timelines. If in the beginning you don't introduce him to your friends, don't want to help him with his To Do List, or don't want to talk about your feelings, you're not moving forward. There will be times when you move forward — feel that compelling force to have your needs met — but then find yourself backtracking. If he's still moving forward, you and he are obviously no longer heading in the same direction. If you find yourself thinking regularly about breaking up but then changing your mind because you have some planned event coming up, like your birthday or Christmas, he likely isn't the draw for you.

If your beliefs and goals are really different from his — so different that you can't support his choices — you may experience conflict, embarrassment and unpleasant surprises in the relationship. We need to keep the ones we love *safe* from harm and free from pain. If you choose a guy who has wildly different beliefs from yours, you might experience the negative consequences of his choices (when he gets drunk and drives, for example, or fights or loudly alerts the world to his unpopular, jarring opinions). If your boyfriend embarrasses you in front of friends, if you find yourself hiding rather than sticking up for him, if you can't meet your need to protect him, if you can't keep him safe from the harsh criticism of others, if you can't feel proud of him, if you have to make excuses for him, if deep down you don't even feel he deserves your protection, then these Frog experiences are drawing you away from him.

Check the items on your Hurt List. Do you find things like "not interested in my appearance around him" or "no longer enjoy getting ready to go out with him"? If so, you've stopped meeting your need to feel alive. If you see items like "I don't do special things for him anymore because they feel too much like work" or if you're simply not making choices that add to his happiness, your need to please is going unmet.

i like myself when i'm with him

You must take care of yourself first — even when you're with your boyfriend. If you stop meeting your own needs (to value yourself, to become familiar with yourself, to challenge, support, accept yourself and so on), you'll start to feel less capable and confident than you did before you entered the illusion of love. If you ever see in your Hurt List "I'm so behind in my life" or "I don't even know where to start to catch up," you've stopped meeting your need to be in control. If you see items like "I do things I later regret, like not paying my bills on time or missing deadlines at work," you're not meeting your need to be financially safe.

♡ HEART-SAVING SHORTCUT: Write out your To Do List, then step back and look at it while remembering that you have to meet your own needs while you're with your boyfriend. How much time do you spend taking care of your own needs, as opposed to doing stuff to meet his needs or satisfy his pet wants? Do you honestly think there's a good balance here?

Somewhere in the middle of your relationship you might begin to make heart-over-head choices to keep your boyfriend happy—that's what Natalie did with Ethan—or you might become nasty if he says hurtful things you don't understand or that seem unfair. To get your boyfriend to meet your needs, you might become clingy, jealous, needy, anxious—even mean. You might choose to do things you normally wouldn't (like having sex before you're ready, doing drugs, or drinking and driving). If this is happening to you, you should be telling yourself, "I can't be with this guy; I'm becoming someone I don't recognize—or like."

i like him as a person

Just as you have to know who you are to find out if you truly like yourself, you have to become familiar with your boyfriend to really know if you like him. Once you become familiar with his traits—with who he is—you may recognize that he can become controlling, or jealous, for no reason. If your Hurt List contains items like "He doesn't say what he means," "He doesn't do what he says" or "He doesn't know right from wrong," you'll know he doesn't use character to get his needs met from you.

Your boyfriend may not be meeting most of his own needs. He may not even have a To Do List to help him meet his need to be financially safe by ensuring he takes care of basic stuff like a job, food and shelter. If so, you might find yourself meeting the needs he should be meeting himself. Then again, you might not mind a life with a slob or with bill collectors following you from town to town. Because of his failure to take action on his own behalf, you'll become controlling in order to "save him." Croak! This is life with a Frog. If you stay with this guy, you won't be able to build the life you want and you won't get to be with a Prince one day.

i am the draw for him

Hurt List items will appear when your boyfriend isn't getting what he's shopping for at your boutique. If you're not the draw for him, you'll hear it in his words and see it in his actions within each of your four needs groups. Because he won't be shopping at your boutique to meet all his needs, you'll feel your own needs — to be accepted, desired, interesting — not getting met.

If you're not the draw for your boyfriend, you'll experience confusion and anxiety about your relationship. If your boyfriend tells you his intent — his vision for your relationship — yet you don't see him moving through the three signposts of his invisible timeline while you *are* moving through yours, you have different expectations. Often a guy will move through his invisible timeline but then begin to backtrack. When this happens, you'll see Hurt List items that link to needs that used to get met. These Hurt List items tell you he's moving away from the relationship. Remember what happened to Natalie?

In the middle of her relationship with Ethan, she wanted to go back to the beginning because the needs she got met then were no longer being fulfilled.

If you don't both believe in supporting each other's To Do List, or using a shared To Do List to find the delicate balance where you're both being helped and pleased, there will be conflict in the relationship. Your roles are to support each other and add to each other's happiness. If your boyfriend isn't supportive of your To Do List, or of the other relationships in your life, he must *become* so or you should stop seeing him. An unsupportive guy is probably also disagreeable, selfish and difficult to get along with unless he gets his way. In other words, he has Frog warts!

If your Hurt List includes "When I ask him a question he says, 'I don't know' or 'I don't want to talk about it right now,'" then your boyfriend's not valuing you. If it contains items like "He never tells anyone about my accomplishments" (for example, doesn't tell other people that you just got accepted to university), you won't get your need to have someone to be proud of you met. If your list contains items that relate to your feeling unimportant, especially when he uses the "if sentence" a lot when making plans ("If we're still together, we'll do this"), you have unmet needs. If he doesn't notice that your brakes are squeaking, yet your girlfriend's boyfriend pointed out that you need new brakes, he's not meeting your lifestyle need to be safe. If he isn't the kind of guy who checks to make sure your bike is properly secured on the back of your car — it's the first time you've used a bike rack — well, you get the point.

You're shopping for a guy who uses good judgement and watches out for you. If on your Hurt List you see, "He drinks and drives and goes 80 miles an hour in a 30-mile-an-hour zone (with me beside him)," he obviously won't meet your need to feel protected and safe.

we're not on standard time here

Hurt List items will tell a girl when she or her boyfriend is not clearing her bar — when there are unmet needs. There's no easy way of knowing right away if your needs are going to get met. But we *can* clear up the issue of *when* in a relationship you should expect to get those needs met. Just be sure your Hurt List items aren't about wishful expectations based on your favorite fairy tale or the last romantic movie you saw with your girlfriend. Nor should you think that passing your six-month or one-year anniversary automatically gives you the right to get all your needs met.

Our expectation of when things should happen in a relationship has to do with our quest for love. We have expectations about how quickly everything should move to happily-ever-after. These expectations are reinforced in the early days of dating, when the guy is romantic and warm and attentive and you fall blissfully into the illusion of love. Right away you want to fast-forward to the middle of the relationship, fantasizing about attending special family gatherings together, going on romantic vacations and being the center of attention at parties, where the world can notice his love for you. You probably assume he has the same expectations because his charms are turned on full.

Then while playing the daisy game, looking to confirm your expectations in your guy's actions, like how many times he calls in a week — or a day — kaboom: your pet wants don't get satisfied. When he doesn't call for three days or doesn't ask you to his best friend's going-away party, your feelings get hurt. You start to think he might just be another Frog (at least until he surprises you with the announcement that he has two tickets to Saturday's game). Until they turn into red flags, your Hurt List items aren't always a reliable indication of whether your pet want is linked to a need.

Relationships often unfold differently from how we expect them to. All relationships have different rhythms and patterns that emerge and evolve over time. We all have needs, yes, but there's no standard timeframe for when we deserve to get them met. Our needs aren't met all at once; they get met, like everything else wonderful in life, over time and through hard work. We have to earn the fulfillment of our needs by building a shared compatible experience with our boyfriend.

In all relationships, you constantly give and receive new information. In the learning loop (needs-choices-consequences), we make new and different choices when we get new information. New information may lead you to either continue or exit. Even if you meet your dream guy and he thinks you're his dream girl, you might not experience a happy ending. Neither of you can predict the future. Love isn't only a feeling; it's something that you can *see* develop as your boyfriend earns it from you over time, doing what he says he will and investing in meeting your needs in all of the needs groups.

Even if your relationship begins with the guy completely smitten, the crazy roller coaster ride will probably slow down as you end up following *his* invisible timeline. If he hasn't introduced you to his mom three months into the relationship, it means he doesn't want to. And that means he's still your *new* boyfriend, not your boyfriend

Let's set your bar with this needs question: is my relationship with my boyfriend similar to my relationship with my best friend? If you answer no, not yet, lower your bar! The needs you expect a new boyfriend to meet are similar to those you expect a new girlfriend to meet. It's too early in the relationship for you to have "entitlement expectations" for how your boyfriend should act toward you. What should you expect? That your guy respect you in the way he treats you and the way he chooses to get his needs met from you.

Until a guy moves through his invisible timeline, he doesn't love you even if he tells you he does — even if he thinks he does! The time and energy he's willing to invest in meeting your needs are the currency he's willing to give you to get what he needs. If he's still at the beginning of his invisible timeline — hasn't introduced you to his friends yet — assume that's where he wants to be. There's no reason to see hurtful signs in your boyfriend's actions, because the way he's acting has nothing to do with the daisy game and everything to do with his invisible timeline. There are times when *it's not about you*. If he's moving too slowly for you, you have the option of respectfully withdrawing and seeking your real Prince.

We all should expect our boyfriends to meet our needs, but often we're also shopping for what we want, not just what we need. Let's look at your lifestyle need to be helped, when the Hurt List item should really be on his list, not yours. For example, you ask your boyfriend to take care of something on your To Do List — in other words, to satisfy one of your pet wants. He has a choice: to satisfy or not to satisfy. To make that choice, he'll evaluate your pet want to determine if it's reasonable. Of course, any pet want is reasonable as long as the other person wants to meet the need to which it's linked and still respect himself or herself.

Let's say on Ella's Hurt List there was an unfulfilled need (to be helped) resulting from a conflict between her To Do List and Ethan's. Ella wants Ethan to pick her up in the morning during his usual workout time. Meeting the need to stay in shape is important to him, and early morning is the only time he can fit a workout into his schedule.

ETHAN: Don't you want me to be healthy?
ELLA: Of course, but can't you do your workout another time?

ETHAN: No, first thing is the only time I can fit it in.
ELLA: If I was important to you, you'd pick me up.

Pet wants create confusion in relationships. Here, Ella's unsatisfied pet want shouldn't be on her Hurt List. Why not? The answer lies in her bar. According to the dating beliefs, she and Ethan both deserve to have their needs met, but not necessarily all their wants satisfied. In a relationship, you're each responsible for building your own life, taking care of your own needs and thus growing happy. Neither one of you should feel pressured to give up fulfillment of your own needs in order to prove the other is special to you. Just as you must take care of yourself first, your boyfriend must look after himself first.

So set your bar with this needs question: do I expect my boyfriend to put me above himself? Generally, your answer should be "No." You deserve to have all your needs met, yes, but you're not *entitled* to have them met. It's like Avril Lavigne being nominated for a Grammy. Maybe she did a lot of hard work, and maybe she deserves to win, but she's not entitled to win. Your boyfriend may not satisfy one of your pet wants because of circumstances beyond his control or because he can't satisfy it and still respect himself. On the other hand, he may simply not want to satisfy it, and that's his choice. So while we expect our boyfriends to make our lives easier by doing favors for us — and that's fine — you're not *entitled* to them being done. If you still feel your boyfriend must absolutely satisfy this pet want for you, even after he's already said no, you've identified an unmet need. So pout, add sugar, or do whatever else it takes, respectfully, to get that need met.

To recognize that you're asking your boyfriend to meet one of your needs when in doing so he cannot respect himself, your bar needs to be set just right. If your boyfriend asks you to do something that requires you to put his needs ahead of yours, he isn't necessarily being disrespectful. The choice of whether to comply is your own. Each of us must find that delicate balance between meeting our boyfriend's needs and meeting our own. It's okay to sometimes meet another's needs while sacrificing fulfillment of our own. So when is it reasonable to give up your own needs in order to meet someone else's? It depends on the need, of course, but also on how frequently the person is asking you to meet that need. Say, for example, that Ella was asking Ethan to drive her to some appointment and he had to miss one workout in order to help her. That sounds pretty reasonable to me — does it to you? It should. But still, it would be up to Ethan to decide whether it was reasonable to him or not.

In the example above, working out fulfills Ethan's need to notice and feel good about himself, a need that he chose to meet in order to grow happy. Here, Ella's attempt to get him to satisfy her unreasonable pet want — because she believes it's linked to her need to be helped — is disrespectful. If Ella pursued her campaign, she would make Ethan's Hurt List hard to manage. In this situation, it's Ethan who'd be suffering a Frog experience.

It can be hard to nail this part — to meet a boyfriend's needs while still respecting ourselves. Your bar will not only help you make a choice but to confirm one. After Natalie told Sean that she wouldn't go to a raucous party with him, she experienced the consequences. Now Natalie will use her bar to figure out if Sean's need is reasonable or not. As we go along here, remember the learning loop (needs-choices-consequences).

UNDERSTANDING HERSELF AND HER NEEDS Natalie has figured out what she needs to be happy. She wants to become a lawyer, and maybe then a judge, and she wants to continue going out with Sean.

MAKING CHOICES BASED ON THAT UNDERSTANDING She made a choice not to go to a party with Sean so that she could study for an exam. When she said she wouldn't go to the party, she experienced Sean's angry and hurt feelings because his need to feel important was not being met.

EVALUATING THE CONSEQUENCES OF THE CHOICE Natalie must first make sense of Sean's feelings, and then stick to her decision or, if necessary, make a new choice. As Natalie thinks about why Sean got so upset, she realizes that he hasn't been as supportive lately of her busy school schedule. Sean has chosen a career where he doesn't have to go to university, so maybe he doesn't see how important it is to her to get great marks. If his Hurt List item is really about the two of them having very different To Do Lists — hers having urgent items to get done each semester with not much time for a shared To Do List, his with few items on it — conflict will result. She wonders if their goals are similar enough and whether or not Sean's resentment of her studying may grow into a red flag.

Natalie talks it through with him. He tells her that he supports her in becoming a lawyer and that he loves her but he can't understand why she can't take an evening off now and then. It makes him feel that he's not the draw for her. When Natalie thinks about it, she realizes that this is true and that Sean does have a good point: she isn't spending enough time with him.

TAKING DIRECT ACTION IF NECESSARY Natalie now has to use her bar to make a choice that includes both their feelings and needs. After all, she's happy almost all the time in the relationship. She decides to meet Sean's need to go to the party.

ADJUSTING YOUR SELF-KNOWLEDGE AND NEEDS Natalie's new choice allows her to be responsible to her life and to build on her relationship with Sean. Including Sean's feelings and needs in her choice. They're both happy. Her bar feels just right.

When a boyfriend hurts our feelings, or we become anxious to fill a need and the chance for filling that need may be slipping away, we can become unfair. If you act on these feelings without taking a little time out first, you can easily make regrettable choices. Of course you feel anxious to do something — anything! — to fix these feelings *right now*, and you likely feel the need to throw harsh consequences at your boyfriend because you're hurt.

In these situations, your Hurt List items are best written down and put in a drawer overnight. This sounds like a stupid idea until after you experience the consequence of striking out at someone; then you wish you'd kept those feelings in the drawer. The next day, take your Hurt List items out. Read them carefully. Do you still feel as hurt and angry as when you wrote them down? If you do, they're probably legitimate and you should take them seriously. If you don't, you wrote them in the heat of the moment. You'll be glad you gave yourself a good night's sleep to calm down and look at things more rationally. This is a great way to fix or manage your own feelings; what's more, you've avoided calling your boyfriend to dump your hurt feelings into his lap, expecting him to fix them. When we're feeling hurt, only Superman would have a hope in hell of jumping over our bar.

It's so easy to get hurt by your boyfriend, because you're much more sensitive to how he acts or what he says than you are with friends. If your girlfriend tells you she'll call you later but doesn't, you probably won't feel hurt. If your boyfriend does the same, you probably will. When we're hurt, a boyfriend can rule our thoughts until he fixes whatever it was he did (or we imagine he did).

Let's take a look at Elizabeth's choice to get her pet want satisfied. While Jordan is out with his friends, she calls him. He's busy, so he tells her he'll call her later. He doesn't. Elizabeth jumps to the (false) conclusion that Jordan was flirting with another girl and forgot about her. The next day she hits him with a harsh consequence — a break-up.

Let's look at Elizabeth's cut-off-her-nose-to-spite-her-face risk/reward choice. *Need*: she's angry and hurt because she thinks Jordan's actions mean "He loves me not!" Her need to feel that she's important to him was not met. This is the only item on her Hurt List, but it's a big item right now! *Choice*: she has to choose what she thinks will meet her needs. She's jealous and angry, so she pokes Jordan with her break-up stick. *Consequence*: later, she feels sad; she misses him. She didn't think through her actions. The break-up stick only helped her to feel better momentarily. She treated Jordan just as a nasty Frog would to get her unreasonable pet want (to feel loved) satisfied. She wasn't being fair because she didn't check to see if the consequences matched his crime.

If Elizabeth had been using her bar to make and check her choices, she could have called Jordan to ask him why he didn't call her back. She could have valued him and explained her feelings, saying, "It makes me think I'm not important to you when you say you're going to call and don't." Or she could have used this simple good-point stick: "I don't like it when you don't do what you say you will." Jordan doesn't talk like a Frog; he'll get it and apologize for his honest mistake (temporary thoughtlessness). Of course, if you often have to punish your boyfriend to get what you need, it could be that you're with a Frog. But it could also be that you aren't using character to get your own needs met. In this case Elizabeth's actions couldn't clear her own bar.

In the learning loop, Elizabeth's *experience* — the consequence of her cut-off-her-nose-to-spite-her-face risk/reward choice — could guide her to avoid making this same choice again in the future. She needs to go back and look at the dating belief "I am the draw for him" to make better rules for making and checking her choices. For starters, she can stop linking Jordan's lifestyle needs — what he does in his life to be responsible (to be important) and have fun (to be pleased) — directly to the daisy question ("He loves me, he loves me not"). She has to get better at managing her hurt feelings in her relationships, thinking through what her feelings mean before she acts. ("Could it be that my hurt feelings are about me and not about him?")

Generally, we can't take one little-picture experience and use it to magically turn any one of the four big-picture dating beliefs into a mistaken belief. For example, the insecure voice in Elizabeth said, "He didn't call me, so I'm not the draw for him." It's difficult not to jump to false conclusions. When we get hurt, we not only say crazy stuff and act like drama divas, we also use *twisted* information to hit others with some unfair harsh consequences.

If you respect yourself, you'll teach your boyfriend how to treat you. Respectfully challenge his words or actions with rules you've made from the dating beliefs; these rules are your standards. "Three strikes and you're out" is a good guideline — especially in Ethan's case; after all, he used up all three strikes in the first few months of both of his relationships.

Using consequences to show your boyfriend how to respect you is a sure way to tell if you're dating a Frog. Even a Prince might need a little help understanding your needs; after all, guys aren't mind readers! When a Prince experiences your consequences, he'll respect and learn from them; a Frog won't get it. But treating your boyfriend disrespectfully won't teach him how to treat you. It's never okay to hurt someone just because he hurt you. In Elizabeth's story, Jordan didn't intend to hurt her; he just lost track of time having fun.

To develop great filtering skills, you must move beyond the me-me world, where you act in ways that include only your beliefs, feelings and needs. While we make choices to get our own needs met, we must understand that our choices affect others, too. When you're dating a guy, your choices affect both of you; so do his choices. A me-me world has no place in a compatible relationship.

To build a relationship with a Prince, you must be able to clearly explain to your boyfriend how he isn't treating you with respect. If you can't tell someone how to respect you, you won't be able to manage your Hurt List. If you're with a Prince, you'll use your bar to work through your hurt feelings, resolve them and move forward to build a relationship. If you're unable to do these things, you'll experience life with a Frog.

Many of us don't know why we stay with Frog boyfriends. To start with, you must believe you deserve a Prince before you can choose one and accept one, or leave a Frog in order to find one. In the next chapter we'll find out how to leave a Frog even if we don't yet quite believe that we deserve a Prince.

FIVE: frog boot camp

Everybody needs to know when to exit a relationship. Knowing when and how to leave can be more important than knowing when to get into a relationship. The last thing you want is to be trapped with a Frog, feeling hurt and confused. It's easy to get trapped by mistaken beliefs ("If you kiss a Frog often enough, he'll turn into a Prince"). But nobody's kisses can change a Frog into a Prince, and if you think a Frog is going to change because he loves you, you're sure to be disappointed — or worse.

Right now, do you think your bar is set too high? Well, if your list of pet wants is too long or if you're too choosy — you give the guy a character exam and expect references — you'll figure out sooner or later that you have to reset your bar. No guy will live up to your standards. On the other hand, if you choose to give up satisfaction of any pet want, not because you can still respect yourself and grow happy but just because you have intense feelings for your boyfriend, then your bar is set too low. The guy you're with is such a Frog that you have to set your bar to "zero expectations" to stay with him.

There's a place in the maze where you can get stuck between "Do I stay?" and "Do I go?" If you're caught in this place, you're lost in love (and not in a good way). Knowing when to exit is important because being with a Frog long enough can leave you feeling stuck, trapped or afraid, as if no action you take will make any difference. If you find yourself in that spot, do whatever it takes to get out. Every minute you stay makes leaving harder. If you're too confused to make sense of your relationship, if you love him and if you don't yet have a bar that is set just right, you need Frog Boot Camp.

Frog Boot Camp serves one purpose: to give you a way to exit your relationship when you're stuck between "Do I stay?" and "Do I go?" What every girl needs is a boot camp to help her set a little bar for the fulfillment of each of her emotional needs — if those needs aren't getting met, she can go!

Dating should be a wonderful experience — not every minute, of course, but in the big picture it should be sweet. As you move toward the middle of the relationship your experiences will change. If you start feeling ongoing hurt, disappointment, confusion or doubt after the happy beginning, you probably picked a Frog. Your boyfriend's actions are not clearing your bar. Somehow he managed to slip through your filter, which you use to identify his warts or your unmet needs. You also might have had needs that were different from those you thought you had (as in the pink-top experience).

In any relationship, you deserve to get your needs met. Gwen's in a long-distance relationship. In both long-distance and regular relationships, you must get each of your emotional needs met, but you *can* choose to give up fulfillment of any of your physical, intellectual and lifestyle needs. In giving up fulfillment of any need, you must still be able to grow happy; that is, find a substitute way of meeting that need by satisfying a different pet want. In any relationship — long-distance or not — when your needs are not getting met they show up on your Hurt List. Your bar will help you see the difference between a genuine need and a pet want.

Gwen's had to fine-tune her bar to be able to judge whether or not her needs are getting met. There's not much fine-tuning required for her emotional and intellectual needs, however, as all those lovely, intense conversations online or on the phone are how she gets those needs met. Conversations are where we do our hardest work to get our needs — to become familiar, to value, to accept, to challenge, to listen, to support and so on — fulfilled. Gwen doesn't get these needs met face-to-face, of course; she talks on the phone or on MSN and shares pictures on Flickr or MySpace or Facebook.

In a long-distance relationship, conversations are even more important, and often more intimate and intense. Without body language to refer to when we talk in person, we need to be that much more precise and expressive when we're communicating long-distance. Generally speaking, if you can't have a heart-to-heart conversation with your boyfriend, he's probably not the guy for you.

Gwen has had to adjust her bar to help her judge whether or not she's getting her physical and lifestyle needs met. This has been hard — different from a regular relationship because experiencing an unmet need often refers not to how one of her pet wants links to a need, but to frequency — how often that pet want gets satisfied. For example, Gwen's had to lower her bar for her physical needs as she only sees her guy on visits or during planned vacations. She doesn't have this unmet need on her Hurt List because she's a low-touch person. Meghan is a different case entirely. When Ben moved away, Meghan tried to keep their relationship going, but she's a high-touch person and couldn't find a substitute for the nearness of him; the lack of physical affection appeared on her list so many times it became a red flag. She had to do something about it. They broke up.

Gwen has had to lower her bar for her lifestyle needs too. She can't expect that her pet wants will be satisfied whenever she wants them to be. For instance, she'll have to give up the shared To Do List that itemizes what each enjoys doing together and what they'll do to help each other. Her boyfriend can still please her, help her, and meet her need to feel important by planning vacations, making visits, sending emails, making phone calls, sending flowers, yakking on MSN and so on. In her lifestyle area she'll also have items on her Hurt List similar to those in a regular relationship, like his not emailing her as often or calling as much as before, or canceling visits with her.

She'll have a lot of Hurt List items resulting from needs not getting met as often as she'd like. Some pet wants that she'll crave to have satisfied won't be reasonable, however, as her boyfriend *can't* satisfy them, and for good reason: he lives in a different city. She'll either accept this and suck it up, or she can exit and find herself a nice regular relationship.

Gwen will have to add a signpost to her long distance boyfriend's invisible timeline: his willingness to talk about how the two of them can live in the same city one day. Until this conversation takes place, he hasn't moved through his invisible timeline. He's still Gwen's new boyfriend.

When you choose to adjust your bar, you'll end up with unmet needs. Any woman in a long-distance relationship will have to do a lot of work to meet her own needs and find substitute ways to have her unmet needs fulfilled. Genuine needs refuse to be ignored.

Let's go back to the regular kind of relationship. Do you love your boyfriend? Does he love you? Most of us would answer these questions with a yes. But there's a difference between having feelings of love and truly loving your boyfriend. To get — *really* get — your big-picture love need met, you must regularly experience getting every one of your needs met — as they come up, of course.

When our boyfriends don't treat us right, we feel it and we know what's going on. Yet we're often reluctant to admit it. We hope that true love will overcome our Frog experiences.

Remember, life can be less confusing with a Hurt List and the learning loop (needs-choices-consequences). Pay attention to your choices and how they make you feel afterward, because each experience creates a consequence: a need met (good feeling) or unmet (bad feeling). After any little-picture experience, you have the chance to reset your bar, and this is how you end up with a bar that's just right. After a while in a relationship, determining whether your boyfriend is the right guy for you gets a lot easier. Being armed with dating beliefs and deliberately looking at your experiences will help you develop a bar for any of your needs. This is how you come to see, feel and think your way through the differences between a genuine need and a pet want.

To set your bar to determine when a pet want is a need or just an extra goodie you can live without and still grow happy, ask yourself: "Can I give up... (insert your specific pet want) and still respect myself?" Say the pet want is bling (diamonds and pearls) and the need is to feel loved. And say you expect bling from your boyfriend on your birthday or Valentine's Day and you don't get it. If you're disappointed, the bling is just an extra goodie. If it stays on your Hurt List, it *does* connect to your need to feel loved.

If you do get bling, it's because your boyfriend *wanted* to give it to you and *could*. Now, say he wants to but can't afford it, ask yourself: "Will doing without bling stop me from growing happy?" Whether you answer yes or no will depend on your own pet wants. You'll find that some of your unsatisfied pet wants will give you reasons to exit and some won't.

Be careful, though. If you're really all about extra goodies, rather than pet wants that connect to genuine needs, you might not have moved beyond the me-me stage of life. You might feel entitled to have others meet your needs, simply so you don't have to — or maybe it's that you don't think you can? If this is the case, you risk sacrificing yourself — your *self-worth* — for anyone who will make you feel loved, even for just a few moments, in exchange for pet-want currency.

Say Elizabeth's boyfriend gives her purely practical gifts. To her, bling indicates how much Jordan loves her. Because she really loves this guy, she's forced to ask, "Will I still feel loved and grow happy getting no bling?" Her answer is yes. This question-and-answer process teaches her about herself and her own needs. Nevertheless, it's still important for her to get birthday bling, so she finds another way to get that extra goodie: she buys it herself. Elizabeth then waits to see if not getting this pet want satisfied by Jordan will show up on her Hurt List again at Christmas — it doesn't. As you become more familiar with yourself, you get a reward: the skill to set and reset your bar.

When you don't feel clear in a relationship, it can be hard to make a deliberate choice to exit. This will make it easier: if you can answer each question below with "Yes," you're with a great guy; if you can't, you're with a Frog. Exit!

- Can I tell him what I really feel — my deepest darkest secrets?
- Can I forgive him when his actions make me really angry?
- Are lots of my needs still met by myself, my friends and family?
- Can I tell my best friend the good, the bad and the ugly experiences I've shared with him without her asking, "Why are you putting up with that?"
- Can I list his two best and two worst traits?
- Can I accept his permanent Frog warts?
- Does he accept me for who I am?
- Does he talk to me like my best friend does?
- Does he avoid using my mistakes to get his pet wants met from me?

Ella can't answer "Yes" to all these questions — Ethan is a Frog for her. She recognizes that Ethan, her frog boyfriend, is not the guy of her dreams — and breaks up with him.

Did you recognize that those were needs questions, which are based on information from the four dating beliefs? Put simply, if *all your emotional needs* are met (your need to be familiar with a guy and have him be familiar with you, to accept and be accepted, to forgive and be forgiven, to value and be valued), you have a great shot at a compatible relationship. If not, head for the nearest escape hatch because with this guy you have zero chance of getting to the fairy tale that is possible! Good luck, Ella.

Using your little-picture experiences you can find both met and unmet needs. Now let's set your bar with your emotional needs within each of the dating beliefs so you can determine with confidence if they're getting met or not.

he is the draw for me

To meet your need to value your boyfriend, you must feel confident enough to tell him what you really feel and think. In other words, you must not fear that he'll tell your secrets or reject you because of what you tell him. Time to set your bar. Can you tell him what you really feel — your deepest darkest secrets? (We're not talking about traumatic things you'd only tell a counselor or doctor.) If you can't, you're not valuing him. Your need to value may connect to any one of the following pet wants: to be able to confess to a lie you told him earlier or a secret about your past, or to be able to tell him you don't like it when he does something and why it hurts you.

Any little-picture experiences that hurt your feelings must be discussed and then taken off your Hurt List. Only then can you meet your need to forgive your boyfriend. Time to set your bar. Ask yourself, "Can I forgive him when his actions make me really angry?" Positive experiences don't cancel out negative ones, even when there are lots of great experiences. You'll know you haven't forgiven him if you can't get past a hurtful experience, if you remain really angry at him for that Hurt List item. If you can't forgive and forget his nasty deeds — the cheating he's done, for example — you must exit.

If your boyfriend wrongs you, you may find it hard to act respectfully toward him. When we get hurt we often act like Frogs ourselves and try to hurt back. Don't. You know the difference between right and wrong because you have character. Anyway, even Frogs deserve respect. You can't have a boyfriend you can't treat with respect. If you're with such a guy now, make a graceful exit.

♡ HEART-SAVING SHORTCUT: Why do boyfriends cheat? First, if a guy is a cheater then the relationship is all about him: his views, his needs, his ways. It follows that he's a guy who makes choices with no concern for your feelings and needs. His cheating choice is a hurtful example of the choices he's been making in your relationship all along! Second, if he does cheat, he's not getting what he needs in the relationship, whether it's because he's a bad shopper, he makes bad choices, or you don't stock what he needs. It's simply about him — not you!

i like myself when i'm with him

Do you feel comfortable with yourself and your choices? If you can't answer yes, you've probably stopped meeting your own needs first. Let's set your bar: ask yourself, "Are lots of my needs still met by me, my friends and family? Or would I feel empty and lost without my boyfriend?" If the latter applies, you're not taking responsibility for meeting your own needs and you've disconnected from other important relationships in your life. You're expecting your boyfriend to make your life complete.

Mistake! Will you still like yourself if you cancel plans with girlfriends every time he calls to ask you out, then lie about why you can't go out with them? Will you still like yourself if you stop getting your needs met with character — no longer saying what you mean or being dependable to others (girlfriends, parents, workmates, schoolmates)? If you start lying to your girlfriends so they won't leave you out of their future plans, will you still like yourself then? Your lying will have consequences: your girlfriends will eventually stop valuing you, stop understanding your situation and stop calling you.

You may find yourself feeling jealous — not wanting to share your boyfriend's attention with another girl or his friends. These are twinges of jealousy — feelings of doubt about how much he likes you. To stop jealousy in its tracks, your thinking voice should say to you over and over, "I'm a great person and any guy would be lucky to have me." After all, you know yourself, so you know that any guy really *would* be lucky to have you. If you become jealous because of something he does, like taking another girl to a movie, talk to him. Ask him his reasons for making that choice. If you're comfortable with his reasons, then talking to him was a great way to stop jealousy in its tracks. If you find yourself trying to change his actions because you're jealous, it has to do not just with his actions but also with how you feel about yourself — your own self-worth. In fact, it may have nothing to do with your boyfriend at all; that is, unless he's a flirting, cheating Frog.

Let's set your bar. Ask yourself: "Can I tell my best friend the good, the bad, and the ugly experiences I've shared with my boyfriend without her asking, 'Why do you put up with that?'" If your answer is no, the message is clear: you don't respect yourself, so you cannot meet your need to accept yourself.

If you're comfortable with your choices and you believe you should respect yourself but also accept your boyfriend's

Frog words or actions, there's a gap between your words and your actions. What does this gap tell you? That your bar is set to accept Frogs. That you don't believe you deserve a Prince! If you don't reset your bar — your standard for how you expect to be treated — you'll probably remain stuck in this relationship, or continue to date Frogs even if you do escape. And what really sucks is that until you respect yourself, Frogs will continue to track you down and ask you out. Frogs have radar for detecting girls who don't respect themselves.

i like him as a person

The first step in determining whether you're with a Frog or not is to become familiar with who he is as a person, independent of you. Learning who he is will help you understand what he needs from you and whether you're prepared to provide it. Likewise, knowing who he is independent of you will help you see whether you can expect him to meet your needs.

Some classic examples of Frog warts will help you identify the experience of life with a Frog. Let's give your boyfriend the same test you gave yourself in Chapter One. Fill in the table on the next page by putting a ✓ beside the traits you think best describe him.

See which traits you identified and then choose his two best and two worst. Did you put a ✓ beside "Jealous," for example?

Our bar is often mistakenly set to this standard: when we see our boyfriend become jealous, we use his jealousy as a "slam-dunk" answer to the daisy question. It's not. Jealousy and mistrust are not signs that he loves you; they're warning signs. Remember the life-is-a-mirror idea? Well, your boyfriend's feelings of jealousy, especially *strong* ones, are like the mirror hitting you over the head and saying "Danger! Frog alert! Head for nearest exit!"

_he's_...

○ Moody	○ Even-tempered	○ Daring
○ Outgoing	○ Shy	○ Easygoing
○ Critical	○ Demanding	○ Outspoken
○ Patient	○ Excitable	○ Sociable
○ Funny	○ Enthusiastic	○ Affectionate
○ Selfish	○ Unselfish	○ Thoughtful
○ Stubborn	○ Confident	○ Opinionated
○ Generous	○ Quiet	○ Open-minded
○ Organized	○ Controlling	○ Focused
○ Popular	○ Honest	○ Assertive
○ Energetic	○ Lazy	○ Jealous
○ Creative	○ Passionate	○ Courageous
○ Sweet/Nice	○ Kind/Warm	○ Sensitive
○ Aggressive	○ Frustrated	○ Angry

A boyfriend who's *always* jealous and controlling and *never* trusting is showing you he feels he's not worth your trust. His lack of self-worth makes him afraid of anything that might take you away from him — your friends, family, a job, other guys. He may even try to manipulate you away from friends and family to tie you more tightly to him.

If you believe your boyfriend's jealousy means he really loves you, you'd better hold up the mirror and look at the two of you. You'll see a jealous guy who, deep down, believes the only way you'll be with him is if he controls you. Worse, you'll see yourself standing beside someone who doesn't believe he's worth much. So what does that make you — his booby prize?

Think about it. This guy doesn't respect himself, so how could he respect you? If deep down he thinks he's not worth much, yet you've chosen to date him, what does that tell you about your choice? If you let him control you, your willingness to be controlled confirms what he already believes: that you don't respect yourself enough to stand up to him and leave. So don't let a jealous Frog manipulate you. If your boyfriend shows extremely jealous or controlling behavior, leave — no, *run away.*

Did you put a ✓ beside "Stubborn"? Or beside "Open-minded"? If you and your boyfriend can have a respectful conversation, you'll be able to get what you want and need from him. Most transactions in a relationship take place during conversations. Conversations are where you bargain for your needs, ending up either with a great deal or getting ripped off.

Like a lawyer, you're in charge of putting together your own defense case for any of your needs. This is your set of good-point sticks for why you think your need is reasonable. Yet talking about your point of view with your boyfriend will be harder than with anyone else. Because you're extra-sensitive around him, just his respectful disagreeing with your points and stating his own point of view can hurt your feelings. If he has Frog warts — like stubbornness — these conversations will be even more hurtful. Work hard at listening to what he's saying and controlling your reactions. You might feel like interrupting him to defend yourself, but don't push the panic button. Just listen. Ask questions to understand his point of view, then present your needs case to him.

Natalie's just made plans to help Meghan move on the last day of the month. She's giving Sean a heads-up that she's going to be busy that evening.

NATALIE: I'm helping Meghan move Thursday.

SEAN: Well I'm not. I just moved Jim.

NATALIE: No one's asking you to.

SEAN: Anyway, you can't help her.

NATALIE: I wasn't asking — just letting you know.

SEAN: No way, I've planned a surprise for you.

NATALIE: Why didn't you mention it before?

SEAN: It was a surprise. You don't believe me?

NATALIE: You always say that — when you don't want me to do something.

SEAN: What favors does Meghan do for you?

NATALIE: It's weird you never notice all the things she does for me. But I'm —

SEAN: (Butts in) You know what? I need help that night. Aren't I important to you?

NATALIE: Yes, you're important to me. Why do you care if I help Meghan move?

SEAN: Which one of us is more important to you?

NATALIE: Why don't you answer my question?

SEAN: Why don't you answer my question?

NATALIE: Ribbet!

Open and respectful communication isn't possible because Sean refuses to listen to Natalie's point of view or to the information she gives him. In the learning loop, such a boyfriend won't meet your need to be heard, so you can't expect him to adjust his self-knowledge to include your point of view. His consequence? He won't learn and grow to make better choices next time. Your consequence? You won't be able to work through your Hurt List items. So your hurt feelings will fester and make you feel frustrated and sad.

You'll become an expert, like Natalie, at recognizing Frog-speak, since you'll be fighting over and over for the right to get any one of your needs met. At the same time you'll sink under the weight of a huge, hard-to-manage Hurt List instead of hanging out and having fun. A big part of building value inside ourselves is teaching our friends and boyfriends how to treat us well. If your boyfriend is stubborn, he won't change his opinion or choice when given new information (such as your point of view). Since we negotiate needs fulfillment in conversations, you'll notice a pattern in your Hurt List: conflict and rerun arguments.

Let's look at the Frog wart experience called invalidation. This kind of Frog wart is easier to spot if you already understand what invalidation looks and feels like, perhaps from having hurt someone else. It's Valentine's Day, for instance, and you're full of happy thoughts for what treats await you from your boyfriend. You get a call in the afternoon, and he tells you he has appendicitis and might need an operation. Boo hoo! When you hang up, what do you do? A) Call your girlfriend and say, "Why do things like this always happen to me?" B) Call your boyfriend back to quiz him on how he's feeling to make absolutely sure he still can't take you out as he promised. C) Call your boyfriend back to see if there's something you can do for him.

If you picked B), you've invalidated someone else's feelings. Elizabeth did! Finding yourself comes with a big, sweet reward: once you understand more about how you get your needs met, you can sit back and *observe* and *recognize* how others do it. Let's put the wart on the other Frog: when a guy doesn't include your feelings or needs in his choices, he's invalidating you.

Here's an example. Sean has just picked up Natalie. They're going for dinner, but they haven't picked the restaurant yet.

SEAN: What do you feel like?

NATALIE: I'm starving, anything. What do you feel like?

SEAN: Chinese. (Heads for the freeway)

NATALIE: Where we going?

SEAN: A new place I heard about. The food's supposed to be fantastic.

NATALIE: (Thirty minutes later) Sean, can't we just pull off so I can grab something quick — at McDonald's?

SEAN: Why?

NATALIE: I told you, I'm starving. I'm getting a headache. My blood sugar's crazy. I haven't eaten today.

SEAN: C'mon, relax. It's not my fault you didn't eat today.

NATALIE: I just need something to tide me over.

SEAN: Hang in, will you? We're almost there...

What seems like hours later, they finally pull into the parking lot. Natalie's *really* angry with Sean. As soon as they sit down, she calls the server over, says she's starving, and orders three yummy dishes. The waitress brings one quickly. Natalie wolfs some food down, still not speaking to Sean. Finally, she turns to him.

NATALIE: Sean, I told you I was starving. Why did you choose a place an hour away?

SEAN: I thought it would be fun to take you to a new restaurant.

NATALIE: You wanted to come here for yourself — not for me.

SEAN: Come on, I said I thought it would be fun! Can you just get off my case? with this?

NATALIE: The waitress got that I was starving — why didn't you?

The discussion goes round and round until he drops her off and she says bye bye, which probably gets drowned out by the door-slam! He never apologizes for not including her needs in his choice of restaurant. Driving away, he thinks, "How ungrateful was that?" This guy can only see his own point of view.

Let's look at the Frog wart "dishonesty." After spending time with your boyfriend, have you discovered a gap between who you thought he was and who he really is? An important part of getting to know a guy is finding out whether you can trust what he says. It's common to trust him right off the bat, but you need to start asking if his words are matching his actions. Your boyfriend's words set up the storyline for what you expect to happen in your relationship. Pay attention to the gap between words and actions, between his storyline and how he treats you. Here's a hint: if other people don't trust your boyfriend, you'll probably find out that you can't trust him either.

Let's look at how Elizabeth's Jordan sets up a storyline, and then how Elizabeth muddles through it. For example, when Jordan told Elizabeth "I love you," she expected that Jordan was saying what he meant. Her expectations were set: she'd be important to him; he'd treat her differently from others; he wouldn't flirt with other girls; he'd call her just to see how she was doing or what was up. Then Elizabeth got busy, so at Meghan's party Jordan flirted with another girl. When she asked him about it, he said, "Maybe if you paid more attention to me, I wouldn't flirt." So she thought, "Huh? I'm not the draw for him He loves me not?." She thought back to how he had treated her on Valentine's Day, with treats and trimmings. "He loves me!" Then there was that humongous crazy argument they had last Friday. "He loves me not?" What's Elizabeth to think?

There are gaps between what some guys say and what they do. As you're getting to know a guy, you have to take what he tells you as the truth, but take it with a heaping spoonful of skepticism. Imagine being surrounded by an invisible shield that protects you until you know your boyfriend has character; only then can you give him the benefit of the doubt. It's up to *him* to remove your shield, which he does by being honest and following through on what he says. If your boyfriend's words or actions don't reach your bar, your hurt feelings will end up on your Hurt List. If he acts like a Prince, he has character. He knows himself. You can trust him. You can forgive him for honest mistakes because they will be just that. If he acts like a Frog, he has little or no character. You can't trust him. You should exit.

Frog warts — like jealousy, disrespect and lack of character — should send you to the nearest exit. But you can't make choices based on little-picture experiences — situations that leave you feeling either happy or confused and sad. These statements seem contradictory. But they're not! Boyfriends aren't perfect, and each guy, like each of us, will have a little part of him that's tricky or confused. So, let's clear up the gray area. If once in a while your boyfriend says "brainless" stuff he doesn't mean, like Jordan's "…I wouldn't flirt," you're not experiencing life with a Frog. If once in a blue moon you experience arguments best described as two Frogs in a battle, where you both behave badly and you both wish you could erase your *own* Frog warts from memory, you're not experiencing life with a Frog.

If, on the other hand, classic Frog warts appear frequently, your boyfriend is using disrespect to get his needs met by you. Let's reset your bar for your emotional need to be able to accept your boyfriend, warts and all. Ask yourself, "Does my boyfriend have Frog warts that I can predict?" You can answer yes if there are Frog things he says or does again and again. We all have good and bad things about us that others will like or not like. So the question is whether you can accept his permanent Frog warts (not whether his good things outweigh the bad). If not, the guy you thought might be your Prince has turned out to be a Frog.

Should Elizabeth trust Jordan? She believes she can't predict Jordan's Frog warts; his confusing actions appear to be isolated incidents. He's not dishonest. He's usually "in her face" saying what he means; afterwards he follows up by doing what he says. Yet she's not sure what all of her Jordan experiences add up to. For example, Jordan can be *very* Prince-like. But last week she found herself forgiving Jordan over and over again for not calling her when he said he would; that is, until he started looking to score some sexy-kitty time. He loves me? Not? Argh!

If your boyfriend often promises to do something but doesn't, he either forgot (an honest mistake) or lied to get what he wanted or misled you because he doesn't know himself well. Whatever the reason, he promised something he couldn't deliver. There's really no difference between a guy lying and a guy changing his mind without a damn good reason. Frogs set up a storyline for you that just won't happen.

A guy's motives — the intention behind any of his tricky or confused warts — don't matter. You don't have a crystal ball, and without one you won't be able to find the truth — as you certainly won't find it by asking your Frog boyfriend. What matter are his actions. When they're telling you that you're not in a safe, respectful, comfortable, fun relationship — that you can't trust him — it's time to exit.

We all have beliefs about how people should treat us (although we might not fully realize what those beliefs are). And we all have the power to change those beliefs. If you've accepted Frog behavior, you can choose not to do so anymore. Do you believe you know and like who your boyfriend is as a person, independent of you? You should believe that you do; if not, you're experiencing life with a Frog.

You deserve to go out with a guy you trust. You deserve to be treated with kindness and respect. If your boyfriend invalidates your feelings, punishes you when you don't do what he wants, says negative things about your body, your intelligence, your friends, or your family, if he gets angry and calls you names like "bitch" or "slut," hit the eject button. Some Frog warts are deadly serious and shouldn't clear any woman's bar. If your boyfriend hits or pushes you or is physically rough in any way, call 911, and then do whatever it takes to find a way to EXIT!

i am the draw for him

For a guy to meet your need to be loved, he must earn your love with his actions, meeting your needs one at a time. Whenever you make an investment, it's okay to want something back. In relationships you're supposed to invest your time and energy to get your needs met. Like you, your boyfriend should invest his time and energy meeting your needs simply to add to your happiness. If you're investing in your boyfriend and he isn't investing in you, a fundamental problem exists. You may love him, but he doesn't love you. Hard as it may be, it's time to exit.

If your boyfriend doesn't want to become familiar with you, accept you, talk to you about his feelings or forgive you, that's his choice. If he chooses not to invest his energy in the relationship, he obviously knows himself and he doesn't love you. If you use information from this dating belief, you can erase your blind spots and — poof! — turn yourself into one smart cookie.

Ask yourself, "Do I know what his two favorite and two least favorite things about me are?" If you don't know, how can you believe he knows and likes you? In any relationship we gather and give information about who we are and what we think about the other person. If your boyfriend doesn't know you well enough to tell you what he likes or doesn't like about you, he isn't becoming familiar with you. Back to the Frog pond he goes.

Let's set your bar. Does your boyfriend try to change you in many ways? If your answer is yes, slap yourself silly! For a guy to meet your need to be accepted, he should mostly accept you as you are. Relationships can help you change and grow, but you don't want to become someone else's pet project, or worse, date someone who thinks you need to be rescued. Guys who want you to change are teaching you how to dislike yourself.

Some guys set up their own little Dream Girl Boot Camp for their girlfriends. A girl in a guy's Dream Girl Boot Camp can feel as if the relationship is all about being molded into his dream girl. Daily life starts to feel like military training: lose weight, dress differently, cut your hair a certain way, wear more makeup, less makeup — you get the picture. Even if you do as he demands, nothing seems good enough. The more you try to please him, the more orders he gives you and the more critical he becomes. He may even say that if it weren't for him telling you what to do, you wouldn't survive a single day!

These commands can be shouted or whispered, given blatantly or merely suggested. Either way, your Frog general creates a gap between who you are and the ideal he expects you to become — and naturally puts himself in charge of closing that gap. And guess what? He'll *never* close it. Dream Girl Boot Camp is about control, not change. There are few things as soul-destroying for a girl.

If you feel your boyfriend is critical of every little thing you do, use your bar to help you to tell the difference between useful criticism, which is offered by someone who respects you, and hurtful criticism, which comes from someone who doesn't. While you're still trying to become familiar with who you are, making this distinction may be hard. The more you know yourself, though, the easier it becomes to take criticism from others, select what is true and useful, and disregard what is not.

If you don't feel your boyfriend knows and likes you as you are, you won't get your need to be accepted met at his boutique! In the next chapter, the question "Do I feel my boyfriend accepts me for who I am?" changes to "Am I sure that I'm not living in his Dream Girl Boot Camp?" You need to be sure, because it's impossible to graduate from Dream Girl Boot Camp.

How do you meet your need to be valued? Your boyfriend tells you what he feels, answers your questions and asks you for what he needs. Let's say he doesn't want to meet your need to be valued, to talk to you about how he feels, or even to answer your questions. Can you accept that your need to be valued is unmet and still maintain your self-respect and grow happy in your relationship? Is it one of those pet wants that is really an extra goodie for you? If it is, you can give it up and still respect yourself and grow happy. But that's unlikely. If your boyfriend won't talk about what he feels and thinks — especially about you and your relationship — he doesn't value you. He's emotionally unavailable. You won't meet your need to be valued at this guy's boutique.

Does he talk to you like your best friend does? Your best friend tells you what she thinks and feels and answers your questions honestly. Having a conversation with your boy-friend should feel as good as having a heart-to-heart conversation with your best friend. Think of how good it feels to talk to her; these conversations make you feel valued, don't they? They probably make you feel as though almost all your emotional needs are being fulfilled, even though just one of your needs — to be valued — is being met with a gold medal.

For a guy to meet your need to be forgiven, he must avoid using your mistakes to get his needs met from you. Let's set your bar. Does he avoid using your mistakes to get you to sat-isfy his pet wants? Often Frogs gather up hurt feelings caused by our mistakes and hoard them in a savings account, taking them out whenever they feel like getting one of their wants satisfied. There's a difference between using a bulleted list to make great points and using another's past mistakes and the guilt that *sticks* to those mistakes to get anybody to do any-thing for you.

Your best friend is just that because of who she is and because the two of you help meet each other's needs. She's not perfect — she doesn't do everything you ask, doesn't always give you what you wanted on your birthday, and so on. But she meets your emotional needs, and perhaps other needs as well. Her friendship helps you feel valued and accepted. You can tell her what you feel and think, and she can do the same with you. When you can, you try to meet one another's needs. Any pet wants that don't reflect the fulfillment of a genuine need will be secondary. For instance, you wouldn't choose a best friend just because she satisfied your succulent pet want for her to drive a really fancy car instead of an ordinary one. If you choose a best friend who meets your needs and whose needs you meet, why would your standard for choosing a boy-friend be any lower?

Boyfriends come and go. There is a beginning, a middle and an end to dating. (The end could be happily-ever-after, or an exit from the relationship.) So there's no reason for you to get lost in love and settle for a Frog. Yes, there's the odd girl whose high-school sweetheart later becomes her husband, who early on finds someone she can learn and grow with. But those cases are rare. If you think the guy you're with now is the man of your dreams, yet you often feel hurt or disappointed in the relationship, it's unlikely he's really your Prince.

Any relationship that doesn't meet your needs is a bad relationship. If your relationship doesn't meet both your emotional needs and your boyfriend's, it will never be compatible. A relationship may or may not have the potential to be compatible, but a boyfriend can never have the potential to be a Prince. He's either a Prince at the time you start going out with him or he's a Frog. If you're in a relationship that doesn't meet your emotional needs, you're with a Frog. And like Ella, the best choice you can make is to leave.

Every boot camp has a motto. Here's yours: "I am a strong, smart, beautiful, resilient woman who knows that in my relationship there are two sets of needs to be understood, respected and fulfilled: mine and his. I'm responsible for meeting my own needs; he has to meet his. I have to help him meet his needs; he's responsible for helping me meet mine. If my boyfriend is tricky, confused, or nasty, is deceptive, or hides his feelings, I'll kick him to the curb where he belongs."

Every boyfriend has both Prince and Frog traits. No wonder it can sometimes feel like you're in love with a guy with a split personality (Dr. Prince and Mr. Frog). While Ella's ready to make the call — Ethan's a Frog! — Elizabeth needs more proof to decide if Jordan's a Prince or a Frog. Now that Frog Boot Camp is over and you've fine-tuned your bar, you're more than ready to tackle the big-picture question: "Is my boyfriend a Prince or a Frog?" The Prince/Frog List in the next chapter will help Elizabeth to see, feel and think clearly enough to tell the difference. Remember Meghan? The Prince/Frog List will also help her.

six: the prince/frog list

As women, we're lovely creatures and regularly follow our hearts instead of our heads. We make lots of risk/reward, heart-over-head choices. Ouch! The learning loop (needs-choices-consequences) frees you to make better choices. If your boyfriend choices repeatedly get you burned because you followed your heart or leave you coming up short because you used your head, then you'll probably figure out that you should use both — to make better choices.

Remember your need to be clear and not confused? Until now, we've used your bar to improve your filtering skills, one need at a time. Now you need another tool — the Prince/Frog List — to see the big picture. It will help you understand whether or not you're with a compatible guy who treats you as you deserve, meets your needs and adds to your happiness. Of course, you'll still have to deal with each moment of your relationship, but the Prince/Frog List helps you see, feel and understand what all those moments add up to.

meghan and michael

Meghan's latest relationship begins when she notices Michael. She does a double-take, smiles at him, tosses her hair, meets his gaze — and that wicked little thing happens! Her child-hood fairy-tale starts to unfold the next day when she tells Natalie, "He's the one." Natalie is skeptical. "What makes you think so?" "He's my ideal guy: tall, dark, intelligent, handsome, funny, romantic, fun, adventurous and attentive." Natalie shakes her head. Tall and dark, sure. But how can Meghan tell at this point if Michael is intelligent, funny, romantic, fun, adventuresome…?

The next day, Meghan and Michael begin spending lots of time together, each making plans designed to delight and please the other. Michael surprises Meghan by picking her up and taking her to the park. (She'd told him it was one of her favorite places to sit and think.) They sit on a bench, sipping coffee, talking and laughing about nothing. As Meghan begins to fall in love with Michael, she ignores Natalie's advice: "Don't picture yourselves together — really together — yet." She thinks Natalie just doesn't get how life works. It was love at first sight, and Meghan *can* see Michael in her future. Even when they're in a crowded room she finds him magically and their eyes lock, filling her with longing.

They soon believe they'll be together forever; they both promise they'll do everything they can to make the relation-ship work. Michael tells Meghan he loves her and says things that add excitement and promise to her beginning fairy tale. In a couple of months they settle into the relationship. Michael is moving through his invisible timeline in the same direction as Meghan. One night, however, she meets more of his friends at a party and doesn't particularly like the experience. He acts differently with her around his friends. The next day she talks to him about it.

MEGHAN: So how do you know all those guys?
MICHAEL: Well, the guy who threw the party works with Bill. Why?

MEGHAN: Nothing. You acted different around them, that's all.

MICHAEL: What do you mean? I had a great time.

MEGHAN: I kept hearing, "Hey, remember when we did this or that?" Who's Suzy?

MICHAEL: Half the stories those guys tell aren't true. They're just to keep the ladies amused.

MEGHAN: I wasn't. And I can't see why you and Bill are such good friends — besides, he doesn't like me.

MICHAEL: Why do you say that?

MEGHAN: Well, we've only ever exchanged "Hi."

MICHAEL: He's a big flirt — doesn't want to piss me off. That's why.

MEGHAN: Whatever. Why'd you ignore me last night?

MICHAEL: What do you mean?

MEGHAN: A couple of guys hit on me. Do they even know we're together?

MICHAEL: They were hitting on you because you're cute.

MEGHAN: I felt like I was invisible. Oh, yeah, except for you yelling, "Hey babycakes, grab me a beer!"

MICHAEL: Listen, I got a little carried away. Sorry. I love you, baby. Come here.

MEGHAN: Okay, but don't do that again please. That was disrespectful.

MICHAEL: Bill didn't hit on you, did he?

Meghan's still trying to get to know Michael better. She finds him fascinating and loves the challenge of figuring him out. He remains a bit of a "Mystery Man" to her, often doing what she least expects. Sometimes, it's almost as if she can't wait to see what he'll do or say next.

The work starts when Michael can't see the difference between Meghan helping him with his To Do List — and doing it for him.

MICHAEL: Hey, my Auntie Jo really likes you. Can you visit her again after work today?

MEGHAN: Well, actually…

MICHAEL: And after that, pick up mom's prescription.

MEGHAN: Hello! You want me to do something for you, ask me, don't tell me.

MICHAEL: Sorry, baby.

MEGHAN: You used to check in on your Auntie Jo. Her place isn't exactly on my way home, you know.

MICHAEL: Yeah, but she really likes you…

MEGHAN: RIBBET.

MICHAEL: What's that?

MEGHAN: A Frog sound. Look, we need to chat about the stuff you want me to do.

MICHAEL: Don't you like doing things for me?

MEGHAN: I'm really busy. I can't take over what you're supposed to be doing.

MICHAEL: Elizabeth does everything for Jordan.

MEGHAN: That's her choice.

MICHAEL: She loves to do stuff for him just because she's crazy about him

MEGHAN: Whatever, Michael. I don't have time to make your lunches, do your shopping and clean your clothes.

MICHAEL: Hey, my laundry was just throwing some stuff in with yours. And you make great lunches, baby!

MEGHAN: That's not the point.

It's true that Meghan loves to do things to help and please Michael. But the work continues as she tries to get Michael to understand why he can't always expect her to do him favors — satisfying his many pet wants, all from his own To Do List. After one of their arguments, he gives her a bunch of consequences, like not letting her help him do anything, which drives her crazy. Just the other day they were running late to meet Elizabeth and Jordan to grab a bite, yet Michael wouldn't leave till he made his bed.

MEGHAN: We're going to be late. Let me help.
MICHAEL: So now all of a sudden you want to help me.
MEGHAN: How come you're in a crappy mood?
MICHAEL: You're usually such a bitch about helping me do stuff, I'm just surprised.

Meghan grabs the corner of the bed sheet and starts to fold it over, ignoring Michael's comment.

MICHAEL: Turn the comforter around. It goes the other way. It's not covering the bed right.
MEGHAN: This way?
MICHAEL: Toward me. Don't you know your right from your left?
MEGHAN: I thought you meant my right.
MICHAEL: Turn it counter-clockwise — forget it (he pulls off the bedding to start over). I'll do it.
MEGHAN: Michael, we're going to be late. You're doing this just to get back at me!

More work comes when Michael appoints himself the boss of her To Do List.

MEGHAN: I'm going out with Nat and the girls on Friday night.
MICHAEL: No.
MEGHAN: You're kidding — right?
MICHAEL: I had something special planned.
MEGHAN: You always say that.
MICHAEL: Do not.

MEGHAN: Anyway, I was telling, not asking. It's Elizabeth's birthday.

MICHAEL: I don't care.

MEGHAN: Why don't you like it when I go out with friends?

MICHAEL: I love you, and you're not going to find anybody else who will ever love and protect you like me.

MEGHAN: Mike, you're not listening. Why don't you like it when I go out?

MICHAEL: You don't have enough time to spend with me as it is. Who's more important to you anyway, me or her?

MEGHAN: You're both important.

MICHAEL: Pick one.

MEGHAN: That's ridiculous.

MICHAEL: Really?

MEGHAN: Michael, you're not the boss of my To Do List. I choose what needs I meet and when I meet them, for both you and Natalie.

MICHAEL: Yeah, well, explain to me why you talked and talked to Natalie when she broke up with Sean, yet you were too busy to do me any favors.

MEGHAN: You expecting me to do you a favor is different from Natalie asking me to help her make sense of her feelings.

Trying to keep her happy-ending storyline on track has been hard work for Meghan. As they move into the middle of the relationship, she sometimes wonders if Michael is really who she believed he is. But her doubts melt away when he's back to being his tall, dark, intelligent, handsome, funny, romantic, fun, adventurous, attentive self again. Mostly she loves those little-picture desire experiences when he's affectionate and playful. She feels close to him in a way that's different from anything she's experienced before.

Lately Michael's been going to parties without her. And Suzy, his ex-girlfriend, has entered the story with a deadly grenade in hand. Meghan hears rumors that Michael flirts and makes out with Suzy at these parties. She hopes his friends are just making up stories to break them up because they don't like her.

When she asks Michael how he feels about his ex, he doesn't want to talk. Natalie's told her that Michael is just one of those guys who isn't comfortable talking about his feelings and is only willing to listen to how she feels if her feelings have nothing to do with him — and Suzy is about him. Meghan tries again to talk to Michael about Suzy, but he's sticking to his guns.

MICHAEL: I do tell you my feelings. I've told you I love you.

MEGHAN: Last week when I asked if you liked Suzy, you said "No" but refused to talk about her. I know you hang out with her.

MICHAEL: What, did you check my phone log?

MEGHAN: No!

MICHAEL: We're friends. She just happens to be where I go. Don't you trust me?

MEGHAN: You guys went to a movie last night, didn't you?

MICHAEL: Bill went with us. Who told you?

MEGHAN: It doesn't matter — you didn't tell me. Does Suzy want to get back together with you?

MICHAEL: There's nothing to talk about. Okay? Case closed.

Meghan questions whether they share the same rule: don't cheat. Recently they went on a double date with Michael's best friend Bill, and a girl who wasn't Bill's girlfriend.

MEGHAN: Wow, I haven't seen Julie for ages. It'll be fun to catch up with her.

MICHAEL: Julie isn't going to be there. Bill's bringing another girl.

MEGHAN: Did he and Julie break up?

MICHAEL: Not officially.

MEGHAN: Uh, Michael, I don't…

MICHAEL: Hey, who are we to judge Bill, okay? If you don't wanna go, fine. I'm going. He's my best friend.

Meghan wakes the next morning feeling like something's wrong or missing — her Hurt List is growing. She can tell how much Michael "loves it" when she says, "We need to talk." Somehow those conversations about how she feels start and end with her sounding needy. She doesn't know what he's thinking or feeling because he never tells her. His line is "Relax, baby. Everything's okay. Let's just have some fun." To her this means, "Stop overanalyzing everything." She thinks maybe she should do exactly that. He's happy as long as they're not having these rerun unfulfilled-needs conversations. Besides, he doesn't have any answers to her questions.

Somewhere in the middle of the relationship the fights — such as who gets to pick what to do or Michael's give me/get me demands — get bigger.

MEGHAN: Saturday night I was thinking I'd cook us a nice dinner and we'd watch a movie. Sound good?

MICHAEL: We're going to Bill's. I already told him we're coming.

MEGHAN: Can't we talk about what we're going to do before you make plans for us?

MICHAEL: Sure.

MEGHAN: Baby, we're supposed to do things we both like. Remember sharing?

MICHAEL: Whatever. We have a 50/50 rule — we rotate who gets to pick, remember? It's my turn.

MEGHAN: You just picked! I seem to remember watching golf on TV all afternoon.

MICHAEL: Yeah, and then you picked going to your niece's birthday dinner after that. Don't you remember anything?

MEGHAN: I didn't "pick" that. It was a family event. Besides, you refused to go and went out with Bill.

MICHAEL: It still counts as a pick whether I go or not.

MEGHAN: Michael, you're unbelievable!

MICHAEL: Suck it up, baby. We're going to Bill's.

Even after all this time she still doesn't feel that she knows where Michael's coming from. She's finding it harder and harder to understand him. And now, when they fight, each sees the other as the villain responsible for their disappointments.

MICHAEL: Why didn't you tell me you felt that way earlier?

MEGHAN: I did. You didn't listen.

MICHAEL: No, you didn't. We've always done this...

MEGHAN: Michael, I don't understand you. If you loved me, you'd —

MICHAEL: I do love you.

MEGHAN: Just once it would be nice if you helped me do what I needed to get done!

MICHAEL: What?

MEGHAN: We always do what you want. Never what I want to do...

MICHAEL: You're so selfish. With you it's always "I want, I want." Give me a break.

MEGHAN: What? I just want you to please me, too — do what I like sometimes....

MICHAEL: Give your head a shake.

MEGHAN: We don't have a shared To Do List when everything on it is what you want to do.
(*This triggers an arsenal of bullets representing every
mistaken word or action she's said or done in the relationship. In the blame game, the bullets —"You said..."
"Yeah, well you said..."— come hard and fast. They both
end up wounded.*)

Sometimes Meghan stays in bed, crying — sad and confused, not as alive as she felt before. At other times she cries
in the shower, shakes it off and pushes herself out the door.
Lately she's had to fix her own feelings without as much help
from Natalie as she used to get.

MEGHAN: Michael and I had another fight.
NATALIE: About Suzy?
MEGHAN: No, another stupid argument about what we're
doing on the weekend. Anyway, he and Suzy are just
friends.
NATALIE: (skeptical) What? Anyway, has he called to
make up yet?
MEGHAN: He will.
NATALIE: I don't understand this guy. Doesn't he get it
that you're, like, ten times better than Suzy?
MEGHAN: Sometimes I don't understand him either. But
I'm crazy about him.
NATALIE: Well, I hate to say this, but I just bet he hangs
out with Suzy again, leaving you to find out after the
fact — again.
MEGHAN: Natalie, I know, and I don't like it. But I love him!

She doesn't feel loved as often as she used to, which is hard
to ignore. And Suzy is driving her crazy. To fix the Suzy hurt,
she asks Michael to perform "back-flipping" types of sacrifices —

like "Can you drive me to Seattle to go shopping?" or "Would you wallpaper my bathroom?"—to prove he loves her. He refuses. But there are still times when she does feel loved. Just last night they grabbed some fast food and a picnic blanket and went to sit by the water. The moment was magical. They had a great view of the ocean, the sunset was gorgeous, his kisses were perfect and, well, Michael was perfect.

Still, Meghan still finds it hard to get Michael to understand her. He judges what she says and often takes it the wrong way, accusing her of manipulating him or punishing him. Recently they had another Suzy conversation.

MEGHAN: Michael, did you see Suzy last night?
MICHAEL: Where did you hear that?
MEGHAN: You've said the three of us would go out for — weeks! You're disrespecting me.
MICHAEL: What do you mean?
MEGHAN: You say we can all hang out but we never do. Yet you keep going out with her, ignoring my feelings and breaking your promises.
MICHAEL: I love you.
MEGHAN: If you don't stop going out with her, I can't keep seeing you.
MICHAEL: You have guy friends.
MEGHAN: I've told you what I need. Stop going out with Suzy on your own all the time. If you can't, I have to stop seeing you.
MICHAEL: It's not fair — you're just punishing me because you're jealous of her.

Meghan is going crazy trying to get Michael to see what she wants: to get a reasonable pet want satisfied out of respect for herself, not to punish him. She's so frustrated she feels like screaming. Why can't Michael see it from her point of view?

They both start saying things they regret afterward. Last week when he wouldn't talk about Suzy, she said she hated him and she broke up with him. She immediately regretted it. They've both said so many good and bad things it's hard to keep track, but when Meghan isn't angry at him she pictures herself with Michael forever. As she's thinking about all this her cell rings. It's Natalie.

NATALIE: Wanna go rollerblading tomorrow? It's supposed to be nice.

MEGHAN: Oh! I'd love to. I miss blading with you. I just can't start tomorrow.

NATALIE: Why? What's going on? You sound tired…

MEGHAN: I am a little. I took your advice and spoke to my English prof about the essay I didn't hand in, and he's letting me submit it late tomorrow.

NATALIE: How's it going?

MEGHAN: It's not. Everything's so crazy lately.

NATALIE: Do you want me to help you work on an outline?

MEGHAN: Thanks, but I'm on my way over to Michael's to drop something off for him.

NATALIE: Doesn't he know you have that paper due?

MEGHAN: It's just something quick he needed me to do. By the way, things have been way better with us since I talked to you last.

NATALIE: So you're not going to dump him?

MEGHAN: I love him, Natalie. I know he's not perfect, but we made a commitment. We can work things out.

Some days Meghan is prepared to do the work to get back to the picture of how it was in the beginning. She believes that she and Michael *will* get back to that picture because they're in love. Princes aren't perfect, and she's behaved badly to him too. The important thing is that he loves her and she loves him. She also believes she can teach him how to treat her and meet her needs. She's willing to invest the energy into helping him be more Prince-like.

Getting lost in the illusion of love can be really confusing. It can be a good thing if you're with a Prince, and it feels great most of the time. However, getting lost in love is not a good thing when you're with a Frog. You're sad and confused about what your feelings really mean. And it's almost impossible to make good choices when we're lost in love. What Meghan needs is the Prince/Frog List to help her make a tough heart-plus-head choice.

meghan fills out her prince/frog list

The Prince/Frog List consists of a Prince Section and a Frog Section. Within each section are the four dating beliefs with their corresponding emotional, physical, intellectual and life-style needs.

the prince section

The Prince Section is easy. It has a bunch of needs questions, which are answered with "Yes" (Y), "No" (N) or "Not Sure" (NS). Answering each question in the Prince Section with a "Yes" depends on really understanding what each needs question means. For example, for the belief "I know and like my boyfriend," the needs question "Can I accept his permanent Frog warts?" relates to your emotional need to accept. However, if you didn't understand what *character* meant, your answer could easily be wrong — you'd have a blind spot.

Below is the Prince Section of the Prince/Frog List that Meghan has completed for Michael. She's read each needs question and answered it with a "Yes," "No" or "Not Sure."

prince section

EMOTIONAL NEEDS

Value: Can I tell him what I really feel — my deepest darkest secrets?
Y ⊗ N ○ NS ○

Forgive: Can I forgive him when his actions make me really angry?
Y ⊗ N ○ NS ○

Familiar: Are lots of my needs still met by me, my friends, and family?
Y ○ N ○ NS ⊗

Accept: Can I tell my best friend the good and the ugly experiences I've shared with him without her saying "Why are you putting up with that?"
Y ○ N ○ NS ⊗

PHYSICAL NEEDS

Notice: Do I know why I find him attractive?
Y ⊗ N ○ NS ○

Desire: Do I know what physical affection I enjoy most with him?
Y ⊗ N ○ NS ○

INTELLECTUAL NEEDS

Interested: Can I list his top three favorite things to talk about?
Y ⊗ N ○ NS ○

Listen: Can I have respectful conversations with him?
Y ⊗ N ○ NS ○

Understand: Can I challenge and support his beliefs, goals and choices?
Y ○ N ○ NS ⊗

Proud: Do I willingly stick up for him in front of my friends and family?
Y ⊗ N ○ NS ○

Beautiful Life: Am I working on my own To Do List to get the life I want?
Y ○ N ○ NS ⊗

LIFESTYLE NEEDS

Alive: Do I take extra time to take care of myself?
Y ⊗ N ○ NS ○

Important/Helpful: Do I include his feelings & needs in my choices? Am I helpful with his To Do List?
Y ⊗ N ○ NS ○

Pleased: Do I do *thoughtful* things to add to his happiness?
Y ⊗ N ○ NS ○

Safe: Can I keep him safe from harm?
Y ⊗ N ○ NS ○

HE IS THE DRAW FOR ME

I KNOW AND LIKE MYSELF

EMOTIONAL NEEDS

I KNOW AND LIKE HIM

Familiar: Can I list his two best and worst personality traits?
Y (✓) N ○ NS ○

Accept: Can I accept his permanent Frog warts?
Y (✓) N ○ NS ○

I AM THE DRAW FOR HIM

Familiar/Accept: Am I sure that I'm not living in his Dream Girl Boot Camp?
Y ○ N ○ NS (✓)

Valued: Does he talk to me like my best friend does?
Y ○ N ○ NS (✓)

Forgiven: Does he avoid using my mistakes to get his pet wants met from me?
Y ○ N ○ NS (✓)

PHYSICAL NEEDS

Noticed: Do I know what he finds attractive about me?
Y (✓) N ○ NS ○

Desired: Are we both high-touch or low-touch people?
Y (✓) N ○ NS ○

INTELLECTUAL NEEDS

Interesting: Is he curious about what I think?
Y (✓) N ○ NS ○

Heard: Does he listen to my point of view?
Y ○ N ○ NS (✓)

Understood: Does he challenge and support my beliefs, goals & choices?
Y ○ N ○ NS (✓)

Proud: Does he stick up for me in front of his friends?
Y ○ N ○ NS (✓)

LIFESTYLE NEEDS

Beautiful Life: Does it appear that his To Do List will get him the life he wants?
Y (✓) N ○ NS ○

Alive: Do I see him light up when he makes plans with me?
Y ○ N ○ NS (✓)

Important/Helped: Does he include my feelings and needs in his choices? Does he help me with my To Do List?
Y ○ N ○ NS (✓)

Pleased: Does he do things for me just because it adds to my happiness?
Y ○ N ○ NS (✓)

Safe: Does he keep me safe from harm?
Y ○ N ○ NS (✓)

the frog section

It's our nature to avoid making sense of hurt feelings — our unmet needs — in order to stay in the illusion of love. But when we do this, we're not respecting ourselves. The Frog Section keeps you honest. It holds all the hurt, mixed or disappointed feelings that make up your Hurt List. It shows you the gaps between met needs and those you deserve to get met but don't.

Meghan's first task is to check off, with a pencil, the Hurt List items listed under "He is the draw for me" in the Hurt Feelings Checklist below. She must be sure that all the Hurt List items she checks are red flags, that they do not include isolated incidents or unsatisfied "entitled" pet wants. Meghan uses her bar to make her choices as she goes through the checklist. She must make sure any Hurt List item she chooses doesn't come from feelings of entitlement. If she wants Michael to put one of her pet wants ahead of his, but wouldn't expect that of Natalie, her bar is too high.

hurt feelings checklist: "he's the draw for me"

EMOTIONAL NEEDS

Value: I don't pay attention to his feelings.
Forgive: I can't forgive or forget some stuff.
Signpost: I don't talk about where I am in our storyline.

PHYSICAL NEEDS

Notice: I'm not attracted to him.
Notice: He's less attractive than he used to be.
Desire: I desire affection from him less and less.
Desire: I avoid affection and make up excuses for doing so.

INTELLECTUAL NEEDS

Interested: I don't ask him questions.

Interested: I run out of things to talk about with him.

Listen: I'm not curious about his point of view.

✓ **Understand:** I don't get him — his beliefs and rules.

Understand: I can't support his choices.

Proud: I get embarrassed by what he says or does.

Proud: I look like a fool sticking up for him.

✓ **Signpost:** We have different storylines — we're not moving in the same direction.

Signpost: I'm backtracking out of our relationship.

LIFESTYLE NEEDS

Alive: I don't enjoy getting ready when I go out with him.

Important: I often avoid making plans with him or picking up his phone calls.

Important: I often can't include his unreasonable feelings and pet wants in my choices.

Helpful: I don't offer to help him with his To Do List.

Helpful: He won't let me help him with his To Do List.

Pleased: I don't do special things for him — it feels too much like work.

Pleased: I don't make choices to add to his happiness.

Safe: It's a full-time job for me to fix his bad choices.

Signpost: I don't invite him to hang out with me and my friends.

Signpost: I haven't introduced him to my family.

To fill in Michael's Frog Section, Meghan takes each of the Hurt List items she checked and places it in the dating-belief row under the needs group — emotional, physical, intellectual or lifestyle — that it corresponds to. For example, she's checked off "Understand: I don't get him — his beliefs and rules" and "Signpost: We have different storylines — we're not moving in the same direction," both of which are intellectual needs. These go into the belief row "He is the draw for me," in the column titled Intellectual needs.

frog section ———————————————————————————

	EMOTIONAL NEEDS	PHYSICAL NEEDS
HE IS THE DRAW FOR ME		
I KNOW AND LIKE MYSELF		
I KNOW AND LIKE HIM		
I AM THE DRAW FOR HIM		

INTELLECTUAL NEEDS

LIFESTYLE NEEDS

Understand: I don't get him —
his beliefs and rules.

Signpost: We have different
storylines — we're not moving in
the same direction.

Meghan goes through the same process for the next belief, "I know and like myself."

hurt feelings checklist: "i know and like myself"

EMOTIONAL NEEDS

Familiar: I never used to do "this" (e.g., missing family traditions like my niece's christening).

Familiar: I never used to get this jealous.

✓ **Accept:** I say or do things not lined up with who I thought I was.

Accept: I yell, say things I don't mean in arguments — a lot.

Accept: I've started lying to my girlfriends — more often.

Accept: I accept my boyfriend's Frog warts because I love him.

LIFESTYLE NEEDS

Important: My To Do List is getting harder to manage.

✓ **In Control:** I'm so behind in my life.

Free: I've stopped working toward my goals/dreams.

Safe: I've missed work or deadlines.

Safe: I do things I regret later, like drunken drag racing and so on.

While I've included examples of Hurt List items that connect to unmet needs like important, in control, free and safe, you may also have unmet needs like feeling not as pleased, helped or alive as you did before you met. That's okay, as the items on the Hurt Feelings Checklist are only examples; the checklist is not an exhaustive list of Hurt List items for each belief. Place your own unmet needs in the appropriate row of the Frog Section. Thus, for the unmet need of feeling pleased (because you don't feel as pleased as before you met), put it in the "I know and like myself" row, in the lifestyle needs column, like this: "Pleased: I'm not rollerblading with so-and-so every Saturday like I did before" and/or "Alive: I don't wake up every morning excited about the coming day...where I can fix my difficulties. They seem too big to overcome." And so on. Remember that all of your own needs relate to your big-picture need: a beautiful life.

Meghan goes through the same process for the next belief, "I know and like my boyfriend."

hurt feelings checklist: "i know and like my boyfriend"

EMOTIONAL NEEDS

Familiar: He's ____ (e.g. moody) and I'm ____ (e.g. outgoing).

Familiar: He's often ____ (e.g. jealous) and ____ (e.g. controlling).

✓ Accept: He lies to me about where he was/what he did.

Accept: He doesn't call me when he says he will.

Accept: He doesn't tell me when I hurt him — gets nasty instead.

Accept: He bullies me into agreeing with his point of view.

Accept: I don't like his friends.

Accept: He's a huge flirt — there are rumors that he cheats.

LIFESTYLE NEEDS

✓ Important: He doesn't have a To Do List (not capable).

In Control: He's lost in his life — thinks I'm his life.

Free: He makes it my job to take care of him.

Safe: He doesn't show up for work or class.

Safe: He spends money on fun, not on paying bills.

Meghan goes through the same process for the next belief, "I am the draw for my boyfriend."

hurt feelings checklist: "i am the draw for my boyfriend"

EMOTIONAL NEEDS

Familiar: He doesn't give me the benefit of the doubt.

Accept: He's critical of what I do and/or who I am.

Valued: He won't tell me what he thinks or feels.

Valued: He won't work through his Hurt List with me.

✓ **Valued:** He can't or won't answer my questions.
  Valued: He doesn't pay attention to my feelings.
✓ **Forgiven:** He's like an elephant who never forgets my mistakes.

PHYSICAL NEEDS

  Noticed: He doesn't tell me I look beautiful.
  Noticed: He's critical of my body.
✓ **Noticed:** He notices me less and other girls more.
  Desired: I don't get enough affection from him.
  Desired: He's only affectionate during sex.

INTELLECTUAL NEEDS

  Interesting: He doesn't ask get-to-know-me questions.
  Interesting: He doesn't ask what-I-think-and-feel questions.
✓ **Interesting:** He asks me fewer questions about what I think or feel than before.
  Heard: He doesn't confide in me or take my advice; he ignores my opinion.
  Heard: He doesn't hear my point of view.
✓ **Understood:** He's not happy about — doesn't support my choices of — friends, goals and so on.
  Understood: He doesn't get me, even after I explain.
  Understood: When challenging me, he puts on his Captain Aggressive hat, then attacks.
  Proud: He never talks to me or others about my accomplishments.
  Signpost: He's backtracking out of our relationship.

Lifestyle needs

  Alive: He ignores me around others.
✓ **Alive:** He acts less excited about doing things with me than with others.
  Important: He's always too busy — doesn't call, forgets to call.
  Important: He's so noncommittal about us — if this..., if that...
  Important: He doesn't make enough time for me in his life.

✓ **Helped:** He won't help me with my To Do List.

Pleased: He doesn't know my favorite things.

Pleased: He only does nice things for me when I ask.

Safe: He doesn't watch out for me like he does for himself.

Signpost: I haven't met his friends/family.

Signpost: His friends/family do not support our relationship.

Signpost: We don't use a shared To Do List.

She's done. Wait! Since the items in the Hurt Feelings Checklist are examples of unmet needs, she might still have some hurt feelings that she didn't find a match to. First off, her hurt feelings don't need to be a perfect match to the items on the checklist; similar is okay. Second, it's possible she had Hurt List items that weren't included in the Checklist. Say you have a pet want, which links to a lifestyle need, that your boyfriend doesn't satisfy: when he drops you off at night, he doesn't wait to make sure you get in the door safely. Put this item in the lifestyle needs box in the "I am the draw for him" row of the Frog Section like this: "Safe (from harm): Doesn't watch to make sure I get in the house before he drives off." Say you have unsatisfied luxury pet wants. Place them in the "I am the draw for him" row of the Frog Section, in the lifestyle needs box, like this: "Pleased: No mansions, no bling, he doesn't treat me to meals" and/or "We have to take the bus everywhere"— you get my point.

what does michael's prince/frog list tell meghan about her relationship?

Below are all the needs that Meghan deserves to get met in her relationship with Michael; beside each need is her "Yes," "Not Sure" or "No" answer. If we lived in a perfect world and Meghan was experiencing a compatible relationship with Michael, she'd have answered each needs question in the Prince Section with a "Yes." She didn't.

	EMOTIONAL NEEDS	PHYSICAL NEEDS
HE IS THE DRAW FOR ME	Value: Y Forgive: Y	Notice: Y Desire: Y
I KNOW AND I LIKE MYSELF	Familiar: NS Accept: NS	
I KNOW AND LIKE HIM	Familiar: Y Accept: Y	
I AM THE DRAW FOR HIM	Familiar/Accepted: Y Valued: NS Forgiven: NS	Noticed: Y Desired: Y

The big-picture rule is that when all of your needs get met according to each of the four dating beliefs, you're in a compatible relationship. But since we don't live in a perfect world and relationships do take work, there could be a few "Not Sure" answers and the relationship could still be compatible. The first thing Meghan must do is count her "Not Sure" or "No" answers. She has 14 "Not Sure" answers — too many. Each unmet need equals work — hard work!

The second thing Meghan must do is to write the word "Love" on a piece of paper. Then she has to write out each of

INTELLECTUAL NEEDS	LIFESTYLE NEEDS
Interested: Y	Alive: Y
Understand: NS	Important: Y
Proud: Y	Helpful: Y
Listen: Y	Pleased: Y

Beautiful life: NS

Beautiful life: Y

Interesting: Y	Alive: NS
Heard: NS	Important: NS
Understood: NS	Helped: NS
Proud: NS	Pleased: NS
	Safe: NS

the unsatisfied needs she has listed in the Frog Section on the next page. (Note: in front of each Hurt List item is the need identifier.) Why? Because each Hurt List item in Michael's Frog Section links to an unmet need. Here is Meghan's unmet needs list for her relationship: to understand him, to accept herself, to be important to herself (in control of her life), to accept him, to be with someone who's capable, to be valued, to be forgiven, to be noticed, to be interesting, to see him come alive around her and to be helped.

frog section

EMOTIONAL NEEDS	PHYSICAL NEEDS

HE IS THE DRAW FOR ME

I KNOW AND LIKE MYSELF

Accept: I've told him I hate him.
Broken up with him a million times.

I KNOW AND LIKE HIM

Accept: He lies to me *a lot* about
where he was/what he did.

I AM THE DRAW FOR HIM

Valued: He won't answer
my questions.

Noticed: He notices me less
and Suzy more and more.

Forgiven: He's like an elephant
who never forgets my mistakes.

To get to their happy ending, Meghan and Michael have a ton of work to do in a storyline best described as two Frogs in a useless struggle to get to the fairy tale that's not possible. Not pretty.

INTELLECTUAL NEEDS	LIFESTYLE NEEDS
Understand: I don't get him — his choices.	
Signpost: We have different storylines — not moving in the same direction	
	Important: I'm so behind in my life.
	Not capable: He's lost in his life with no To Do List.
Interesting: He asks me fewer questions about what I think or feel than before.	**Alive:** He acts less excited about doing things with me than with others.
Understood: He's not happy about — doesn't support my choices of — friends, goals and so on	**Helped:** He won't help me with my To Do List.

Meghan will now use her bar to see, feel and think through each one of the four dating beliefs. Should she believe, for example, that Michael is the draw for her and she for him?

he is the draw for me

In the Prince Section, for the belief "He is the draw for me," her emotional, physical, intellectual and lifestyle needs are pretty

prince section

EMOTIONAL NEEDS

Value: Can I tell him what I really feel — my deepest darkest secrets?

Y ☑ N ◯ NS ◯

Forgive: Can I forgive him when his actions make me really angry?

Y ☑ N ◯ NS ◯

PHYSICAL NEEDS

Notice: Do I know why I find him attractive?

Y ☑ N ◯ NS ◯

Desire: Do I know what physical affection I enjoy most with him?

Y ☑ N ◯ NS ◯

HE IS THE DRAW FOR ME

frog section

HE IS THE DRAW FOR ME

much getting met. Meghan answered all of the needs questions with a "Yes," except for one: to understand Michael (see below), which got a "Not Sure." Clearly, she believes Michael is the draw for her — a big draw.

INTELLECTUAL NEEDS

Interested: Can I list his top three favorite things to talk about?
Y ☑ N ○ NS ○

Listen: Can I have respectful conversations with him?
Y ☑ N ○ NS ○

Understand: Can I challenge and support his beliefs, goals & choices?
Y ○ N ○ NS ☑

Proud: Do I willingly stick up for him in front of my friends and family?
Y ☑ N ○ NS ○

LIFESTYLE NEEDS

Alive: Do I take extra time to take care of myself?
Y ☑ N ○ NS ○

Important/Helpful: Do I include his feelings and needs in my choices? Am I helpful with his To Do List?
Y ☑ N ○ NS ○

Pleased: Do I do *thoughtful* things to add to his happiness?
Y ☑ N ○ NS ○

Safe: Can I keep him safe from harm?
Y ☑ N ○ NS ○

Understand: I don't get him — his beliefs and rules.

Signpost: We have different storylines — not moving in the same direction.

"Not Sure" and "No" answers in the Prince Section are often supported by a hurt feeling in the Frog Section. In other words, Meghan's "Not Sure" answer to "Can I challenge and support his beliefs?" gets supported by her unmet need: "I don't get him — his beliefs and rules" in the Frog Section. Meghan sees that her intellectual need to understand her boyfriend is not getting met. This made sense when she remembered how Michael had that whole "Mystery Man" thing going on — she couldn't understand where he was coming from.

Any signpost inside your own Prince/Frog List is like a huge flashing neon warning sign that says "At least one of you doesn't wholeheartedly want to be in this relationship." Signposts tell you you're not on track to get to the fairy tale that is possible. Ouch! Even when we're starting to back out of a relationship, we're often not aware that we are — which is why knowing about signposts is so helpful. If you're truly in love with a guy, you love yourself, you love him and he loves you. Remember when Meghan wrote out the word "Love" and then listed her unsatisfied pet wants from the Frog Section? She had lots and lots of unmet needs! You can tell from her unmet needs list that Meghan is meeting her need to love Michael by sacrificing the needs she's responsible for meeting herself and the needs she deserves to get met from a Prince who knows himself and loves her.

i know and like myself

In the Prince Section, for the belief "I know and like myself," Meghan's not meeting her needs. She answered "Not Sure" to all three needs questions (see pages 158). She might believe that she knows and likes herself when she's with Michael but she shouldn't. Ouch!

If Meghan believed that she must know and like herself, she'd be making choices to meet her own needs—to grow happy. When you ignore your beliefs you create a gap between what you believe and what you do. In the Frog Section her two Hurt List items are: "Accept: I've told him I hate him. Broken up with him a million times" (an emotional need); and "In Control: I'm so behind in my life" (a lifestyle need). The unmet emotional need is a great example of how your Hurt List items don't need to be a perfect match, as this "Accept" hurt feeling is similar to "Accept: I yell, say things I don't mean in arguments—a lot." Until Meghan narrows that gap between what she believes and what she does, she'll find many instances of not respecting herself or others. Meghan has to keep working on her character—to keep practicing to say what she means. Yes, even when she's hurt and angry.

Meghan's becoming busier working on Michael's To Do List. As a result, she's neglecting her own beautiful life. She isn't respecting herself because she hasn't aligned her actions with her belief that she has to take care of herself first. Every day she stays in the relationship she'll become less familiar with herself and feel less capable, less confident and less in control of her life. She'll become needier and more sensitive to Michael's Frog actions, desperately shopping at his boutique to feel better, like a Christmas shopper an hour before closing on Christmas Eve.

Learning how to respect yourself, and then applying self-respect in your life, is a long journey. When we get lost in our life, we stop using a To Do List to meet our own needs; we can all begin to feel as if our boyfriends are our whole lives. Meghan might believe that Michael not only *adds* to her life but is her *whole life*, which might explain how she's ended up feeling that she's not in control anymore and why she's confused about who she is as a person.

Meghan is neglecting her beautiful life because she's too busy doing all the work in her relationship (while Michael's having all the fun). She's hurt and upset about this, but she's hanging on for dear life to keep her hope of love alive. You might shake your head and say "What's wrong with you, girl?" but Meghan is experiencing what many girls go through with

prince section ————————————————————————

EMOTIONAL NEEDS   PHYSICAL NEEDS

I KNOW AND LIKE MYSELF

Familiar: Are lots of my needs still met by me, my friends and family?
Y ○   N ○   NS ☑

Accept: Can I tell my best friend the good and the ugly experiences I've shared with my boyfriend without her saying "Why are you putting up with that?"
Y ○   N ○   NS ☑

frog section ————————————————————————

I KNOW AND LIKE MYSELF

Accept: I've told him I hate him. Broken up with him a million times.

Frog boyfriends. Have you ever had a friend who stayed in relationships even though she spent all her time crying or complaining about that boyfriend? Girls get trapped like this when they want to believe they're with a Prince yet clearly are not! Guys can be just as capable of destroying your self-worth as they are of helping you become familiar with yourself.

INTELLECTUAL NEEDS

LIFESTYLE NEEDS

Beautiful Life: Am I working on my own To Do List to get the life I want?
Y ○ N ○ NS ☑

Important: I'm so behind in my life.

i know and like him

In the Prince Section, for the belief "I know and like him," Meghan believes she knows and likes Michael's traits and how he gets his needs met from her. Should she?

Wait a minute. In the Prince Section, Meghan answered all three of the needs questions with a "Yes." Yet in the Frog Section, there are Hurt List items that contradict these answers. Remember the exercise in Chapter One about your personality traits, the one you also asked your girlfriend to do for you? Think of your Hurt List as your girlfriend, because it challenges you; it either backs up what you believe or shows false your answers in the Prince Section.

Let's look at the needs question "Accept: Can I accept his permanent Frog warts?" and one of Meghan's hurt feelings: "Accept: He lies to me a lot about where he was or what he did"

prince section ————————————————————

EMOTIONAL NEEDS   **PHYSICAL NEEDS**

I KNOW AND LIKE HIM

Familiar: Can I list his two best and worst personality traits?
Y ☑   N ○   NS ○

Accept: Can I accept his permanent Frog warts?
Y ☑   N ○   NS ○

frog section ————————————————————

I KNOW AND LIKE HIM

Accept: He lies to me *a lot* about where he was/what he did.

from the Frog Section. So now we have "My boyfriend uses character to get his way: he lies to me to get his Suzy succulent pet want met." Does this sound right? Sounds like a contradictory statement!

Here's another contradictory statement: in the Frog Section, Meghan's other hurt feeling was linked to Michael's lifestyle need: "Important: He's lost in his life with no To Do List." Yet she answered the needs question "Beautiful Life: Does it appear that his To Do List will get him the life he wants?" with a "Yes." So now we have "My boyfriend's To Do List will get him the life he wants; he's lost in his life with no To Do List."

♡ HEART-SAVING SHORTCUT: The gaps between what needs any girl believes — or wants to believe — she's getting met (Prince Section) and what needs she's not (her Hurt List) help her to see that she's snagged a Frog, not bagged a Prince.

INTELLECTUAL NEEDS   LIFESTYLE NEEDS

Beautiful Life: Does it appear that
his To Do List will get him
the life he wants?
Y ⊘   N ◯   NS ◯

Important: He's lost in his life
with no To Do List (not capable).

You need great filtering skills to see great information. It's our nature to filter what truth we use in our choices. Have you ever heard someone say, "You only heard what you wanted to hear"? Well, most of us do hear only what we want to hear. You see, once we know our truth, our beliefs can change — we can then feel compelled to make new choices that mirror these new beliefs. For example, what if Meghan believed she didn't know and like Michael? Would she keep choosing to treat him like her Prince? Hopefully not!

You'd think that Meghan would have a list chock full of unmet emotional needs within this belief. Yet she doesn't — she has blind spots. In order to judge whether she likes Michael or not, let's look at what Meghan isn't including. Michael definitely has warts — lots of them. We saw how he got his needs met from Meghan: he didn't listen to her, invalidated her feelings, called her a bitch and so on. Remember Frog Boot Camp? Well, Meghan's experience shows you how a relationship unravels when you don't know that your emotional needs aren't getting met, and what happens when you don't recognize who your boyfriend is as a person.

Meghan knows Michael's two best and worst personality traits — she answered this question with a "Yes." This is a good start. However, there are three ways for each one of us to get our needs met, and Michael isn't meeting the needs he's responsible to meet for himself. He makes risk/reward self-gratification choices. When we don't meet our own needs or work through what hurts us, one of the consequences is that we stop seeing anyone else's point of view. Early in the story, Michael tells Meghan to relax, to stop overanalyzing stuff; he can't see her feelings.

Michael's living in his me-me world, shopping at Meghan's store to get his needs met — sounds like a needy and high-maintenance Frog. Doesn't it? He uses the relationship to take care of himself first. He's the definition of a self-centered, selfish person, one who will have a hard time meeting the needs of another. With a guy like Michael, any experience that is supposed to be shared ends up being about him, not about you and him. Needy, high-maintenance Frogs don't ever start shared To Do Lists; they're not interested in finding that delicate balance where your needs and theirs are being met equally. And they think their the boss of a girl's To Do List, so she feels controlled, not free to make choices to meet her own needs.

Even when a guy thinks he truly loves you, if he can only see the world through his own needs filter, the relationship probably won't work. He might be handsome, he might tilt his head to give you that smile that says you're the only one, but none of that matters if his choices are all about meeting his own needs. Michael's not able to become anyone's Prince anytime soon; he has lots of personal development work ahead of him. Until he knows how to take care of himself, it will be impossible for him to take care of somebody else.

i am the draw for him

In the Prince Section, for the belief "I am the draw for him," Meghan's emotional, intellectual and lifestyle needs are for the most part not getting met. She answered almost all questions with a "Not Sure." Her only met needs in the relationship are the needs to be noticed, desired, familiar with and accepted. In the Frog Section, her Hurt List items are plentiful. She doesn't feel valued, forgiven, noticed, interesting, understood, helped or alive. See the match between most of her "Not Sure" answers in the Prince Section and her Hurt List in the Frog Section? (I've put them into italics for you.)

prince section

EMOTIONAL NEEDS

Familiar/Accepted: Am I sure that I'm not living in his Dream Girl Boot Camp?
Y ⊘ N ○ NS ○

Valued: Does he talk to me like my best friend does?
Y ○ N ○ NS ⊘

Forgiven: Does he avoid using my mistakes to get his pet wants met from me?
Y ○ N ○ NS ⊘

PHYSICAL NEEDS

Noticed: Do I know what he finds attractive about me?
Y ⊘ N ○ NS ○

Desired: Are we both high-touch or low-touch people?
Y ⊘ N ○ NS ○

I AM THE DRAW FOR HIM

frog section

I AM THE DRAW FOR HIM

Valued: He won't answer my questions.

Forgiven: He's like an elephant who never forgets my mistakes.

Noticed: He notices me less and Suzy more and more.

Remember the daisy game "He loves me, he loves me not"? Look at the Frog Section row for the belief "I am the draw for him" to find your daisy answer. He doesn't love you unless he's drawn to meet each and every one of your needs as they come up in the

INTELLECTUAL NEEDS

Interesting: Is he curious about what I think?

Y ☑ N ◯ NS ◯

Heard: Does he listen to my point of view?

Y ◯ N ◯ NS ☑

Understood: Does he challenge and support my beliefs, goals and choices?

Y ◯ N ◯ NS ☑

Proud: Does he stick up for me in front of his friends?

Y ◯ N ◯ NS ☑

LIFESTYLE NEEDS

Alive: Do I see him light up when he makes plans with me?

Y ◯ N ◯ NS ☑

Important/*Helped:* Does he include my feelings and needs in his choices? Does he help me with my To Do List?

Y ◯ N ◯ NS ☑

Pleased: Does he do things for me just because it adds to my happiness?

Y ◯ N ◯ NS ☑

Safe: Does he keep me safe from harm?

Y ◯ N ◯ NS ☑

Interesting: He asks me fewer questions about what I think or feel than before.

Understood: He's not happy about — doesn't support my choices of — friends, goals and so on.

Alive: He acts less excited about doing things with me than with others.

Helped: He won't help me with my To Do List.

---

relationship. Until he's willing to do so, even if your boyfriend tells you he loves you — even if he thinks he does — he doesn't.

Like you, your boyfriend has three ways to meet each of his needs. We've already discussed one part of the picture for

Michael: meeting his own needs in the dating belief "I like him as a person." Now let's talk about the other two parts. Michael isn't shopping at Meghan's boutique for the following ("Meghan is the draw for me") needs: to value her, forgive her, notice her, be interested in her, understand her, light up around her or help her. Instead, he's shopping at Meghan's store for favors. He's looking for her to satisfy pet wants on his own To Do List — to meet the needs he's responsible to meet himself. Sounds like Michael believes he knows and likes Meghan as a person; that is, as long as she's doing favors for him.

The third way he gets his needs met is when he feels the effect of Meghan shopping at his store for all of those "He is the draw for me" needs. He's one lucky little Frog: he's loved, valued, forgiven, noticed, desired, alive, important, helped and pleased; there is someone who finds him interesting and who is proud of him. His only unmet need, if he were to really think about it, would be to feel understood (Mystery Man). Meghan is the big loser in this relationship. In the Frog Section she has oodles of unmet emotional, physical, intellectual and lifestyle needs.

Do you see her blind spots — her so-called met needs, and no Hurt List items where there should be? Her emotional needs: she doesn't feel valued (Michael won't discuss Suzy) and forgiven (we saw those he said/she said bullets used in arguments). Yet in the Prince Section she believes Michael is familiar with her and accepts her — he doesn't. Blind spots!

Do you see the contradictions between her so-called met needs and her Hurt List items? Her physical needs: with Suzy in the picture Meghan feels less noticed. Yet in the Prince Section she feels noticed — contradiction! Her intellectual needs: she doesn't feel interesting (actually, in the Prince Section she does — another contradiction) or understood in most aspects of their relationship, including arguments.

Her lifestyle needs: Meghan feels less and less included in Michael's life because he spends less time pleasing her.

Michael's "Love" storyline does not line up with his actions. So Meghan shouldn't believe she is the draw for Michael, nor should she believe that he loves her. Fewer of the needs that were fulfilled at the beginning of the relationship are being met in the middle; Michael is slowly backtracking out of the relationship, yet Meghan has another blind spot because she didn't include this signpost in the Frog Section.

♡ HEART-SAVING SHORTCUT: If you're not the draw for your boyfriend, in the Frog Section you will have at least one unmet emotional, physical, intellectual or lifestyle need. If you still squeeze him through that door of reasonable doubt, you have a bad case of coping amnesia — you're filtering out your life-with-a-Frog experiences. Often when this happens, a woman unconsciously uses her physical needs to arrive at the conclusion she's with a Prince — not because of the quality of sex, but because she believes that sex and affection are the definition of love.

It's up to us as characters in our own personal life stories to decide what we want our beautiful life to look like. So what sounds good to you? A co-starring role in "The Fairytale That's Possible" or a supporting role in the "Princess and the Frog"? Not surprisingly we'd wish the former, but — alas! — wishes are for kids; our own role gets cast after we've chosen a boy-friend — our co-star. The Prince/Frog List helps you to differentiate between life with a Frog and life with a Prince, and it's how you find your answer to *Frog or Prince?* The Prince/Frog List might be exactly what some girls need, just like following a yellow-brick road to find the right decision — if he's a Frog, dump him. Others may end up in a Frog trap: what to do if the guy who's stolen your heart is a thieving Frog and you don't believe you deserve a Prince? In the next chapter we'll see how to escape that nasty Frog trap!

SEVEN: *stuck in a frog trap?*

$\mathcal{D}o$ you need to raise your bar? To be able to recognize and then choose a Prince, you must believe you have value. To be able to recognize, and leave, a Frog — same thing. Without a sense of your own value, you're up a creek without a paddle. Or, to put it another way, you're in a relationship without a bar.

Rather than setting her bar to "Prince Charming," Meghan cut and pasted the image of her ideal guy — her Prince Charming — onto Michael. Yet she doesn't expect Michael to behave like a Prince. Meghan stepped into the middle of her relationship with no real bar and no way to make sure her emotional needs would be met. So she finds herself lost in love and wondering, "Should I stay or should I go?" still making those heart-over-head choices.

Without a bar it's easy to make choices to satisfy a pet want without respecting ourselves. Making bad choices — like Natalie did with Sean — is easy when you don't have the right information about what a guy's Frog warts are. We're not born knowing what invalidation is, for example, so it's hard to recognize the experience of being invalidated.

If you've just been invalidated in a conversation with your boyfriend but don't recognize it, you'll feel hurt and bewildered.

If you recognize what he did, you'll call him on it, pointing out that he should include your feelings and needs in his choices. If his actions were an honest mistake, he'll stop.

Making bad choices is easy when you're unaware of your needs. Meghan believed she was the draw for Michael. Yet Michael's Prince Section showed that he wasn't meeting her needs. What should Meghan do? She can use the dating beliefs to raise her bar by knowing her needs and how she should be treated. She can exit when she sees unmet needs or if she learns that her needs are different from what she thought they were — like Ella did with Ethan when she satisfied his bedroom pet want.

Making good choices is easy when you're aware of your needs. With information from the dating beliefs, you'll be able to recognize and reject a Frog, and recognize and build a relationship with a Prince. Unless you have coping amnesia — that is unless you ignore your boyfriend's Frog warts and your unmet needs like Meghan did. Because Michael was *really* the draw for her, she unknowingly trundled into a Frog trap! Meghan, Natalie, Ella and Elizabeth have all let a guy kiss away his Frog warts — bet you have too. Yet the only cure for coping amnesia is valuing yourself. Tight spot!

are you with a frog right now?

The choice to stay with a Frog is your own. But if you keep thinking that all this stuff about Frog warts is too dramatic and not a good enough reason to break up, you're lost in love. You might also be lost in your life — not a good state to be in. Dump your boyfriend, finish reading the book, then reread Chapter One before you even look at another guy! In other words, you need to stop playing the game of love for a minute. Step back and try to figure out how you ended up being so dangerously lost in love. If you don't, you'll probably end up there again.

♡ HEART-SAVING SHORTCUT: When a girl stops shopping at her own boutique, she can avoid connecting to how she really feels, and before she realizes it she has stopped meeting her own emotional need to value herself. With unmet emotional, physical, intellectual and lifestyle needs her own beautiful life is stark and empty; her consequence is that she starts to shop at her boyfriend's boutique to feel better. Sometimes a girl will use sex or drugs to disconnect from her own empty life and get fleeting moments of happiness. If given the opportunity, she would be afraid even to make eye contact with a Prince.

Just as love can be beautiful, it can also destroy your sense of self, hurt your ability to figure out what you need and steal the energy you require to choose and build what's best for you. You can tell you're lost in love if you find that your boyfriend is ruling your thoughts. You may lose interest in doing what you need to do to take care of yourself. You may stop working on your To Do List. You may find it hard to enjoy things that used to bring you pleasure — like Natalie, who replaced other items on her To Do list with "Ethan this" and "Ethan that."

If you're lost in love, in conversations with friends you might talk only about your boyfriend or you might cry about him. Maybe, even though you're having lots of conversations with your friends to sort through your feelings, their advice is not helping. At some point you might stop talking about your boyfriend, as your excuses for him don't work anymore with your girlfriends. You might become embarrassed that you accept the way he treats you. You may even stop returning friends' calls altogether

If you don't respect yourself enough to exit when you should, the illusion of love can disintegrate into an awful love experience. Every time you make a risk/reward choice to accept unmet needs — and thus not respect yourself — you get hurt and you tear down your sense of value. When you stay with a guy who treats you disrespectfully, you get hurt. When you give your boyfriend what he needs but don't get what you need, you get hurt. You build your value by standing up for yourself and insisting that your needs get met. So if you believe you deserve to be treated respectfully, but your boyfriend doesn't, you'll tell him that you won't accept (insert the type of behavior) because it's hurtful. If he doesn't listen, well, there's another unmet need: to be heard. Aligning your beliefs with how you act means you'd respectfully withdraw — dump him.

meghan's chemistry experience

Meghan believed that Michael was the draw for her and she for him. Yet she was mistaken. She had a big, bad case of coping amnesia. Chemistry played a big role in her story. Meghan wasn't paying attention to getting all of her needs met or to which need had been met with chemistry. When she met Michael, they were both struck with physical chemistry (to notice and to desire) but weren't able to move beyond it to a compatible relationship. Thus she got stuck in the maze between "Do I stay?" and "Do I go?" Michael's actions failed to clear her bar, setting off an inner alarm, and her thinking voice said, "Hey, wait a minute. Is this guy a Frog?" But she switched off the alarm by thinking, "Suck it up. I love Michael. He's all I need to be happy."

Repeatedly her chemistry-charged desire need kicked in: "Come on, you can give up that Hurt List item — after all, I got fulfilled." So she moved along, meeting her own need to be pleased using risk/reward to keep herself happy. Then she started to barter with herself (wrong move!), using her beautiful life needs and the needs she deserved to get met in the relationship. Each time she gave up the fulfillment of a need, she lowered her bar.

Michael didn't help matters. He'd say or do almost anything — croak like a Frog, waltz like a Prince — to make sure his sperm swam free. When Meghan did talk to him about her unmet needs, his words came back to her like a lullaby, rocking her back to the hope of love.

Meghan confused chemistry with love and wanted to believe that Michael loved her back ("He said it! He said it!"). So she didn't use her filtering skills and threw her self-respect right out the window. She ignored his Frog warts and her unmet needs and became a prisoner of love — a slave to her desire need. She easily filtered out Michael's Frog warts using the belief that all is fair in love and war to make and check her choices. She also applied this belief to her own actions — after all, she wasn't always respectful of Michael.

There are two parts to the draw: the first is "one who attracts." Here the attraction is chemistry. The second is "one who holds our interest." To hold our interest, a guy should meet our needs. If he doesn't, we're actually drawn away from him, and your thinking voice whispers "Should I go?" This question is the cue for our filtering skills to kick in and for us to really see, feel and think about why that question arises. Of course, when one of our needs has been met with chemistry, our thinking voice whispers right back, "Should I stay?" And we immediately use our filtering skills to block "No" and shout "Yes!"

Meghan is just letting life happen; she's filtering out her truth, consciously or unconsciously, to stay with her boyfriend. Every choice comes with a cost. If you choose to act on chemistry no matter what, you'll learn the cost from whatever happens next. Chemistry can bring something really wonderful or something really horrible to the next part of your life. Choices based on chemistry alone are just as likely to destroy a person's value as they are to bring love.

You fail to use your bar for a variety of reasons. One might be chemistry; another might be that you believe — deep down —

♡ HEART-SAVING SHORTCUT: One morning you wake up shocked that you suddenly have a huge Hurt List. You wonder what's happening: yesterday he was your Prince. For starters, you haven't been using your filtering skills. The needs you are getting met — to love, value, desire, be interested and so on — are the *only* ones you're shopping for at his boutique, whereas the other needs you deserve to get met within the dating belief "I am the draw for him" are going unmet. Chemistry often transports you here.

that a Frog is all you deserve. First things first: chemistry can cause us not to see a Frog, even when everyone else recognizes him. It is a powerful force that can hit two people when they meet. There's a kind of resonance when they magically sense something familiar in one another. When this resonance happens between people who know and respect themselves, the results can be breathtaking. If you and your boyfriend have both grown up knowing what a healthy, loving relationship looks and feels like, the chemistry you experience can very well develop into the same kind of relationship. If you weren't fortunate enough to grow up in such an environment, then following the dating beliefs can help get you to this same place.

Chemistry can be dangerous when it happens between people who both lack a sense of their own value. These are individuals who haven't been able to meet their own needs and who may have suffered serious harm from drugs, abuse, neglect or rejection. Two people can resonate together when they've experienced similar pain. Pain and chaos can become normal and familiar to a person who has grown up with them, driving him or her to *seek out* chaos and resonating with others who offer it.

Chemistry can attract you to a Frog and keep you with him simply because you believe chemistry is love at first sight, and you believe love at first sight is real love. But chemistry can be like a false-positive pregnancy test — it shows a positive result that isn't real. If there's chemistry, you'll quickly get feelings of love, even though you're not really in love. Only when you truly feel and have experienced *all* of your needs being fulfilled can you say that your need to love and be loved has been met.

Here's a way to check for a false-positive love test result. Before you believe that your need to love is met, fill in a Prince/Frog List. Take a piece of paper, draw a line down the middle and then on the right side at the top write the need "Love." Below, on the left side, list the needs that have been met. (These will come from the "Yes" answers in the Prince section.) Now list the unmet needs you have in the Frog Section. Be sure to cross off those so-called met needs that are contradicted by a Hurt List item in the Frog Section. You should now have, on the left side of the paper, a list of met needs. From this list, you'll recognize one or more of your needs that are getting met in a super-charged way, by chemistry.

The second reason you fail to use your bar is when you believe that a Frog is all you deserve. Your thinking voice can affect whether or not you believe you deserve a Prince. In life you're responsible to teach yourself and others how to treat you, how they speak to you in conversations, and how they get their needs met from you. Until you treat yourself with respect — and this includes training your thinking voice to respect yourself — you'll not necessarily know when others aren't doing so. Do you call yourself a loser when you make a mistake or do something you think is wrong? Do you call yourself fat or ugly when you look in the mirror? Your own thinking voice can award you the consequence of choosing Frogs!

Your best friend can tell you a thousand times that you're not a loser. But only when you train your thinking voice to tell yourself that you're one smart, strong, and beautiful woman, will you start to expect what you actually deserve. Whenever you stand at the mirror, your thinking voice should say, confidently and lovingly, "You are truly gorgeous, girlfriend." You must also train your voice what to say when you make a mistake. Instead of screaming "Loser!" it should calmly say, "Oops! Okay, I'm smart enough to learn from that one and do it differently next time."

Just as your thinking voice may call you stupid or a loser, it may also make disrespectful comments about others. When you call your girlfriend and she doesn't answer, your voice might say, "Sam, you bitch, you never answer your phone!" Train that voice to respect yourself, however, and you automatically train it to respect others. When it stops being critical of you, it will stop being critical of others.

build your value

If you believe you have value but are dating a Frog, you have a mistaken belief. Pay attention to your feelings, which are, after all, poking you in the heart — that heartache, disappointment, confusion and doubt are trying to point you in the right direction to see that unmet need. Paying attention to your feelings is the first step toward believing that you do have value and deserve better. Life is a journey, and you should be walking forward. In the baggage you carry, take all your good consequences. For some it's a career they love, or perhaps a wonderful relationship they've built with their best friend.

Take all your bad consequences too. These may include experiences in which you broke every respect rule — maybe living the *Girls Gone Wild* headlines, or experimenting with sex, drugs and rock 'n' roll. We carry all of our consequences, good and bad, with us as we go. Which is a good thing — a *very* good thing — because consequences teach us some of the most important lessons in life, lessons about who we are, what we need, and how to choose. These lessons help us to see, feel and think we have value. The consequences you carry remind you of what you learned from them. As you move forward, you can build on the good ones while being careful to avoid the bad ones.

To gain your own sense of value, you must look at where you are in the ongoing process of knowing and liking yourself. You have a gap to close between knowing yourself and loving yourself. How familiar are you with yourself, and do you accept what you know? Think back to all the best things people who care about you have told you about yourself. Then review the worst things that people who care about you have told you about yourself. Now step back. Be fair. Remember we all have both positive and negative traits and we've all made some good choices and some really bad ones. Do you accept yourself? Make sure you don't define who you are <u>only</u> by your bad choices. These mistakes are part of who you are, yes, but they don't define who you're going to become. In fact, the opposite is true: you can look back and make sense of your bad choices and know in your heart that you have the ability to make better choices starting today. You just have to stop making risk/reward choices and keep your eye on the learning loop (needs-choices-consequences).

Your journey toward building your value is like finding an exit out of a maze. A maze is complicated, so you're not going to get through it in one day. In a maze, forks in the path are inevitable and you come upon them often. Each time you do, you have to choose a direction. If you hit a dead end, you don't just sit down — you have to keep moving. Each time you choose a direction, you don't have a clue what is in front of you. It could be a dream life, or it could be a booby prize (unmet needs, hurt feelings, life with a Frog). At times, you can feel like you're going around in circles and you'll never exit the maze. Don't give up. You may not realize it, but with each *deliberate* choice you're building your sense of value. Every choice — good or bad — is a step along the way to a beautiful life. Winston Churchill, the British prime minister during World War II, put it this way: "If you're going through Hell…keep going!" So keep moving no matter what. You'll get there.

We're all born with value, but not with a sense of our value. Aligning who we are with what we do builds our sense of value. Meeting our needs and spending time with people who accept us and treat us with respect build this sense of value. Still, like the characters in fairy tales, we can become our own worst enemy, hanging out and making friends with villains. When one of your consequences leaves you feeling there's no hope, keep your eye on the exit and don't lose sight of the big picture.

The learning loop helps you make your best choices. Even if what you should do next isn't obvious, even if you can't figure out the right path in the maze, you can step away from what's hurting you. While you're taking that step, think back to a word or a phrase someone who cared about you told you — something to help you believe in yourself. Whatever the consequence of the choice you just made, you'll learn from it and make a better choice next time. Making that courageous choice, and learning from the experience of the consequence, will be a huge deposit in your self-respect currency account. The learning loop gives you a fighting chance to get to the fairy tale that's possible.

You'll get there. Applying self-respect to each choice is the secret to learning and growing, to gaining self-knowledge. Gradually, you'll align who you are with what you need and how you choose. Even when your life sucks, you can make marvelous progress. It's hard work, but mastering the learning loop is how to close the gap between fully knowing and truly loving yourself. It's the path to the fairy tale that is possible,

and when you master it, opportunities appear along your path.
Sometimes they take the form of a Prince!

♡ HEART-SAVING SHORTCUT: GOLDILOCKS AND CINDERELLA

Remember the way Goldilocks chose what felt just right for
her in the three bears' house? She was choosy with the porridge, the chairs and the beds; she only made choices that met
her needs. Only after she had experienced enough bowls of
porridge and enough beds did she find the right bowl and the
right bed. We all need to be choosy like Goldilocks and not
accept a relationship until it feels just right.

Cinderella not only chose to ignore her evil stepfamily, she
also didn't try to befriend her evil stepsisters — to fix them
with good-point sticks. She didn't lose her way by trying to
change their wicked lazy ways or to explain who she was to
them. Their personal development was their job. If Cinderella
had believed it was her job to fix her stepfamily and teach
them to like her, she wouldn't have had the energy to exit that
wicked relationship and enter a beautiful life that included a
Prince.

Does your boyfriend act or talk to you in the same way
that Cinderella's stepmother or stepsisters did to her? Does he
look at the world through his own needs filter? Like Cinderella,
you can avoid being trapped in a bad situation if, deep down,
you believe you have value no matter what your wicked boyfriend says. Cinderella had the courage and the sense of value
to go from sleeping on her stepmother's cold kitchen floor to
luxuriating in her Prince's palace. She built her value deep
down and increased the chance that chemistry, when she felt
it, meant love. Despite her lowly position and the abusive
treatment she suffered, she had a sense of her value. You see
this by what she does: she defies her nasty stepmother and
goes to the ball, and later she finds the courage to come out of
the kitchen to try on the glass slipper.

the prince/frog list and the big-picture answer: frog or prince?

Once you understand how the Prince/Frog List works and you answer some questions, gather up your Hurt List items and place them into the appropriate belief row and needs group column of the Frog Section, life gets a whole lot easier. Meghan will pass or fail Michael within each of her needs groups to find her big-picture answer. In the last row of the diagram, you'll see that for each group of needs (emotional, physical, intellectual and lifestyle) a boyfriend can only pass or fail. A guy only has to fail one of these to be a Frog. Sound familiar? Think of the exit shortcut at Frog Boot Camp, the one you take when your emotional needs aren't met. Meghan will use her bar to judge whether or not Michael is a Frog or Prince — for her.

She begins at the top of each needs group, starting with her emotional needs and reads down the column until she gets to the last line where it says "Pass/Fail." She checks to see whether or not each of her emotional needs has been met. In the Prince Section, she notes the "Yes" beside the needs to value and to forgive, the "Not Sure" beside the need to become familiar, and so on. Moving into the Frog Section, she notes "Accept: I've told him I hate him. Broken up with him a million times" and so on. When she gets to the last line —"Pass/ Fail," she uses her bar to make sure she can live with any of these unmet emotional needs, be happy and still feel good about herself and the relationship. She has to find the answer within herself.

Meghan repeats this process for her physical, intellectual and lifestyle needs groups in Michael's Prince/Frog List. Can she accept this relationship's unfulfilled needs within each needs group and still respect herself? Or is this guy a Frog who should be returned to the pond?

prince section ─────────────────────

	EMOTIONAL NEEDS	PHYSICAL NEEDS
HE IS THE DRAW FOR ME	Value: Y Forgive: Y	Notice: Y Desire: Y
I KNOW AND LIKE MYSELF	Familiar: NS Accept: NS	
I KNOW AND LIKE HIM	Familiar: Y Accept: Y	
I AM THE DRAW FOR HIM	Familiar/Accepted: Y Valued: NS Forgiven: NS	Noticed: Y Desired: Y

frog section ─────────────────────

	EMOTIONAL NEEDS	PHYSICAL NEEDS
HE IS THE DRAW FOR ME		
I KNOW AND LIKE MYSELF	Accept: I've told him I hate him. Broken up with him a million times.	
I KNOW AND LIKE HIM	Accept: He lies to me *a lot* about where he was/what he did.	
I AM THE DRAW FOR HIM	Valued: He won't answer my questions. Forgiven: He's like an elephant who never forgets my mistakes.	Noticed: He notices me less and Suzy more and more
ANSWER	**Pass/Fail**	**Pass/Fail**

INTELLECTUAL NEEDS	LIFESTYLE NEEDS
Interested: Y Listen: Y Understand: NS Proud: Y	Alive: Y Important/**Helpful**: Y Pleased: Y
	Beautiful life: NS
	Beautiful life: Y
Interesting: Y Heard: NS Understood: NS Proud: NS	Alive: NS Important/**Helped**: NS Pleased: NS Safe: NS

Understand: I don't get him — his choices.	**Signpost:** We have different storylines — not moving in the same direction
	In control: I'm so behind in my life.
	Important: He's lost in his life with no To Do List.
Interesting: He asks me fewer questions about what I think or feel than before.	**Alive:** He acts less excited about doing things with me than with others.
	Helped: He won't help me with my To Do List.

Pass/Fail   **Pass/Fail**

Raising her bar, Meghan fights chemistry — heart over head, love over common sense — and she wins. She fails Michael in her emotional, intellectual and lifestyle needs groups. Meghan, you go, girl!

Michael is definitely not Meghan's Prince. She can't learn and grow in this relationship as there are too many red flags. She has too many unmet needs. Her Hurt List takes too much work to manage; this tells her that she's experiencing life with a Frog. If she stays, she'll be distracted from doing the things she needs to do to build her beautiful life. That distraction is exactly what happens when you're with a Frog. Many girls insist on trying to change or fix their Frog, or they try to make him meet their needs. If you find yourself trying to turn your Frog into a Prince, think of it as a form of Frog abuse. Stop immediately. Be kind to your Frog. Release him so that he at least has a chance to become someone else's Prince!

Having a bar helps you avoid a lot of hurt. Once you set your bar with needs questions from the dating beliefs, the experiences you stumble upon in a relationship become less bewildering. The Prince/Frog List is designed to help you see your unmet needs and then understand what they mean in the big picture of your relationship.

If the Prince Section has "Not Sure" or "No" answers for either the belief "He is the draw for me" or the belief "I am the draw for him," or both, the work is inside your relationship. Remember that you have to be the draw for each other: if he's not the draw for you, you've stopped shopping for fulfillment of all of your needs. The work here is in understanding why he isn't holding your interest and/or why you're willing to go outside your relationship to get so many needs met. If you don't feel you're the draw for him, the work is in telling him what needs he isn't meeting for you. You'll have to sit him down and have a conversation about getting these needs met. Your Hurt List items help you to explain why you feel this way. For example, you might say, "I don't feel important because..." and then list your Hurt List items.

Let's say the "Not Sure" or "No" answers are located in the belief "I know and like myself." In this case, the work is all about you. You have to spend more time and energy becoming familiar with yourself and meeting your own needs with a To Do List. Let's say you have some "Not Sure" or "No" answers in the belief "I know and like him." There's no work for you to do other than telling him what Frog warts he has and that you can't accept them. All the work here — like getting his needs met from others with character, or working on his own life — is for him to do.

Once you've used the Prince/Frog List to answer the question "Is my boyfriend a Prince or a Frog?" and it turns out he's a Frog, you must make the choice to leave. If you do, you're one brave girl. Most of us aren't able to dump our boyfriend cold turkey. We tell ourselves we just need to work harder to fix the problems in the relationship, or that we have to give our boyfriend another chance. ("Yeah, he's got all these Frog warts, but I did make a commitment and I have to accept him warts and all.") But deep down, we know things aren't going to get better. We must leave. To meet our need to be clear and not confused about taking that big step, we need to reset our bar to account for the mistaken beliefs that can keep us spellbound in a Frog trap!

mistaken beliefs

The familiar dating beliefs mentioned in Chapter Three (like "Follow your heart," "Accept a guy, Frog warts and all," "Relationships take work," and "Love is enough") can't be used in a relationship with a Frog. It's too hard to use these beliefs to make respectful choices because you don't use them as they were intended to be used. When you use the learning loop, you learn from each consequence. You make a similar choice next time if the consequence was good, a better choice if it was bad. If you don't connect your experiences to your choices, you can use mistaken beliefs to settle for life with a Frog.

Here's a belief that can add to your confusion: "I must love and accept my boyfriend for who he is, warts and all." This belief is valid in the sense that you can't change your boyfriend's behavior; only he can. So it's correct to believe that if you love someone you have to come to terms with some things — annoying traits or habits — that you may not like. But these warts must not undermine your respect for yourself or for him. You should *never* accept a boyfriend getting his needs met from you like a tricky, confused or nasty Frog, nor should you think you can change that behavior.

Here's another belief that can confuse you: "Relationships take work, and I did make a commitment." This belief is valid, but the heavy lifting is in identifying where your relationship needs work. Doing the Prince/Frog List is constructive; telling your boyfriend over and over again that he isn't meeting your needs is not. Trying to get that need met in rerun arguments is pointless, useless work. At any rate, you've already done the heavy lifting: identifying your unmet needs and talking to your boyfriend about them.

Waiting to get your needs met while fixing your boyfriend is also useless work. So is waiting to get your needs met as they were at the beginning of the relationship. No matter how much work you're prepared to do, you can't turn a Frog into a Prince. If you think you can, it's easy to accept or discount your hurt feelings by giving your boyfriend the benefit of the doubt — making excuses for him like "He didn't mean to do that; he just doesn't know better." STOP! No girl can fix her boyfriend. Even if you could, you are *never* responsible for changing others. You can only change yourself. You do so by adopting different beliefs and creating rules that you live by and include when you make choices.

Here's one more belief that can increase your confusion: "Love is enough to make a relationship work." Not true. Just as affection does not necessarily mean love, love does not necessarily mean compatibility. Following your heart alone will just get it broken for no good reason. You can only follow your heart in a compatible relationship where you use the dating beliefs while respecting yourself and others. When you can do this, you're living in the fairy tale that is possible. What's almost always true is that love is enough when all — *all* — of your emotional needs are met. Memorize this: love, be familiar with, accept, forgive and value yourself and him, and expect the same in return. Only when all of these are met do you have a chance at getting to the fairy tale that is possible.

Yet another belief that can add to your confusion: "If this relationship won't work, I may never find one that does." If you think no one but your current boyfriend would want to be with you, you might stay with your Frog to avoid the consequence of being lonely. Don't. If you stay with a Frog because even though he hurts you, he's the best thing in your life, you're making a huge mistake. There is a Prince out there, but you'll only find him if you have the courage to leave the Frog. Know and respect yourself. Have the courage to meet your needs and build your life. That's what the Prince who's out there looking for you is doing.

Lots of times when you have to break up with a guy, it's not about you; it's all about him. Of course the choice to stay or exit is your own, but if you're not with a guy you know and like, you're not with the right person. Your boyfriend can be the draw for you and you can be the draw for him, but if you don't *like* him or how he gets his own needs met, he isn't right for you. Even if he is the draw for you, even if you like yourself when you're with him and even if you like him as a person, if you're not the draw for him, you're not with the right guy either.

You *must* get your needs met to get you out of the maze and onto the yellow-brick road that leads to the happily-ever-after. You deserve to be with someone who wants to be with you. That's a guy who not only tells you he loves you but earns your love with his actions.

break-up conversation

Breaking up is hard to do, but breaking up with a radar-equipped Frog is especially difficult. What's radar? It's the sixth sense that helps some Frogs find and date girls who are vulnerable — who have no filtering skills and, often, little self-respect. If you've ever dated one, you know how it feels to be with someone who can push all your buttons. During conversations, no matter what you say about your feelings or needs, he manipulates you into believing that his feelings and needs are more important.

Picture a break-up conversation with one of these Frogs. You've thought hard about whether or not to break up. You've talked with your friends. You know this relationship doesn't even come close to meeting your needs; in fact, it may be hurting you in some way. Either way, you can no longer accept this guy's Frog warts or the unmet needs that keep appearing on your Hurt List. You've decided to be strong and end it — to move on.

So you start with, "We keep on having the same arguments over and over. I've asked you to stop calling me names. I've asked you to do what you say you're going to do. I've asked you to treat me more respectfully when we're with your friends. And so on. And so on. We've talked about these things so many times. You say you'll change, but you don't. I've respected you enough to try and help us figure these things out and fix them. I've put as much into this as I'm prepared to. Now that I believe these problems won't change, I need to respect myself and move on."

Some Frogs will listen to everything you have to say. Others will interrupt to defend their position. They'll argue about how you think you should be treated; they'll invalidate your feelings and point of view. But this Frog is different — he has radar. His actions and words will manipulate you so skillfully that you'll be left feeling as if you were completely wrong to think about breaking up. Perhaps he's angry. How dare you break up with him! Or maybe he'll say that you just need to see things from his point of view, which, of course, is the right one. He may even say that you're stupid to see things the way you do.

Maybe he'll play to your sympathy. How could you hurt him like this — he can't live without you! He might say that your list of problems is insignificant compared with how much he loves you. Perhaps he'll shout, break things, even threaten to hurt you if you won't give him another chance. Or perhaps he'll promise to change if you'll just give him more time, citing examples of where he did change (if only for a few days), calling you "baby," trying to kiss it better.

If your break-up attempt goes this way, you'll probably end up feeling confused or guilty. How could your reasons for breaking up make sense one minute and then, after one conversation with your radar-equipped Frog, seem completely wrong? It could be that you wanted to break up because, in your heart, you knew that your Frog was manipulating you. While you were dating, did he seem to know exactly what to say and do to get you to ignore your own needs and place his needs first? Girls who date Frogs like this often reach a point where they can't even remember what their needs were. This is one of the most dangerous places a relationship can take you.

Despite these potential obstacles to a successful break-up, there's good news. If your first attempt leaves you feeling confused, guilty or manipulated, it likely proves that your decision to break up was the right one. After all, no guy worth letting into your life would deliberately make you feel this way — manipulating you is something only a Frog would do. On your second attempt you should probably run the other way as fast as possible — at least until you're safely out of range of this Frog's radar.

Remember that you don't need a guy's permission to break up with him. Nor does it say anywhere that your break-up conversation with a Frog has to end with a friendly handshake or a kiss on the cheek. For many people, respecting their boyfriend means trying to end the relationship face-to-face. If you're one of these people and breaking up doesn't work after a try or two, then it's probably time to just cut and run. At least you tried. Now go ahead and respect yourself: withdraw.

How do you get to be with a real Prince? By figuring out who you are and what you need to be happy; by believing in the value of respect, for yourself and others. By teaching others how to treat you, and then having the courage to exit if they don't treat you that way. By asking your boyfriend to meet your needs and listening to him when he tells you how to meet his. And by choosing to exit if he can't meet the needs that are important to you, or if you can't meet his needs while maintaining your self-respect.

We all need to leave behind a Frog, period. Even though a break-up may lead to the pain of lovesickness, it can also lead to great consequences. What great consequences? In the next chapter we'll find out.

EIGHT: *lovesickness*

As the old song says, breaking up is hard to do. But here's one lovely consequence you'll experience after you send a Frog back to the pond. All the time you've invested in the relationship talking about your Hurt List — which, with a Frog, is very hard to manage — can now be spent on your own life. There's no one to trip you up, to stop you from "the doing," which is exactly what Frogs do.

Here's the not-so-great news: the consequence of a breakup is usually lovesickness. Leaving Frog Guy constitutes an exit from the maze. How hard you struggle to convince yourself that you're free from your past relationship depends on how lovesick you get. It also depends on how strong you are for the task ahead — to put this relationship behind you and move on in your head and heart. The effects of lovesickness can vary from thick, nauseating disappointment and tears to a feeling of extreme anxiousness that cripples you and prevents you from any "doing" — even from eating and sleeping. Nothing pleases you. And almost everything you do — even taking a shower — can seem hard.

Lovesickness can blind you to your needs and make you question the wisdom of breaking up. This chapter will show you how to keep your resolve and turn lovesickness into a positive experience, to reset your bar and, from the four dating beliefs, re-establish or make rules that you won't bend. This chapter is about you — not him. After a break-up, you have to go back and live in your me-me world for a while, making choices that include only your own feelings and needs.

Lovesickness can make you feel like you have to rebuild your life from scratch, but breaking up doesn't actually mean starting again. Each break-up lets you add everything the relationship taught you — about yourself, your self-worth, your needs and your choices — to what you knew before the relationship. You'll be smarter at understanding how a relationship fits into your beautiful life. Everything you've learned will help you answer the big question: how can I find someone more compatible than this guy?

After you break up with a Frog, you'll have a much better chance of picking a Prince. Feeling lovesick tells you that you value yourself, because you haven't ignored your needs just to stay in a relationship that isn't right for you. You've shown that you're strong enough to stand up for yourself. When you do things that show self-respect, you build your value deep down. Breaking up with a Frog is something you do because you believe you deserve to be happy.

Even though you've decided a boyfriend isn't the right guy for you, you'll probably miss him terribly and feel hurt and confused. Being lovesick is about decoupling — getting used to not spending time together. How lovesick you get varies according to where you were in the relationship maze — if he was the draw for you, how much self-respect currency you used in the relationship, how much of your To Do List was about him and how long you were together.

dealing with lovesickness

In the early stages, you may swing like a pendulum from anger to that sick feeling in the pit of your stomach. To make yourself feel better you might lie to yourself or vilify your boyfriend. Don't. Don't allow your thinking voice to say things like "He'll come back to me" or "This isn't over." Don't build your boyfriend a nasty reputation or turn him into a villain. These coping mechanisms won't help you get over your lovesickness or grow happy. When you identify what Frog warts your boyfriend had, or what needs in your relationship went unfulfilled, you're not vilifying him — you're using facts to find your truth.

It's natural to be sad, but remember that you're not mourning the death of a good relationship. You're mourning the loss of the *illusion* of a good relationship. Allow yourself to wallow a bit, but not much more than weeks (as opposed to months) — much longer and you'll risk turning into a drama queen. If you need help picking your spirits up, listen to upbeat, I-can-live-without-you music. Those great in-your-face songs — from "I Will Survive" to "Irreplaceable" — will help do the trick.

A great way to feel better when you're lovesick is to look at your Hurt List again. Review the reasons why you broke up. This will pick up your spirits and help you stick to your decision. You can learn important stuff about a boyfriend *after* you break up. Go over your Hurt List and add any new items that come to mind. This exercise might help you recognize new needs you didn't get fulfilled in the relationship.

Even months after a break-up there may be times when you feel waves of sadness. You might feel as if you're back at day one of lovesickness, but you're not. Thinking about your boyfriend and feeling sad happens less often as time passes, provided you keep building a beautiful life. The longer you're away from him, the more time you'll spend doing your own stuff, not thinking about him.

When lovesickness gets bad, remember this: you had the courage to do what many women simply cannot do. You were brave enough to do something you knew was going to cause you pain, and in doing so you added hugely to your value. And you've given yourself the confidence to know that the next time your Hurt List tells you you're with a Frog, you'll promptly send the little croaker back to the pond.

What if your boyfriend dumped you? Consider yourself lucky: he's done you a favor. In the relationship you tried to determine if your boyfriend was a Prince or a Frog. What do you think he was doing? Any guy who dumps you means you weren't the draw for him. Your guy might have been Prince-like, but he didn't meet those "You're the draw for me" needs, which you deserve to have met. Sounds like a Frog, right? He is! But by dumping you he's freed you from the trap of an incompatible relationship, which was causing you all those hurt feelings. He's also returned you to your To Do List and the building of your beautiful life, and to your girlfriends and family members who were telling you to get rid of him anyway!

Break-up decisions are hard. They hurt. To break up with a Frog you not only have to believe you have value, you have to be strong enough to stick by your choice. If he was the draw for you, you felt as if you got all those lovely emotional, physical, intellectual and lifestyle needs met. Whether you actually did doesn't really matter; your boyfriend won't be around anymore to meet whatever needs he did meet in the relationship.

Slap yourself silly. You deserve more than a discount shopping experience at your boyfriend's store, where finding what you need is hit-and-miss. A Prince's store, on the hand, is like a designer boutique. At a Prince's store you're more likely to find a well-stocked inventory to meet your needs. In fact, this store even carries stuff to satisfy your luscious pet wants. And besides, shopping to find blazing love and to grow happy is what you're supposed to be doing. While shopping for clothes at discount stores is smart, bargain hunting for boyfriends isn't! It's shopping for any guy just to get a boyfriend.

Every day you stay with a Frog you pay with lost self-respect. How much? Just look at your Hurt List — that's how much! Frogs can distract us from the doing in our lives. We invest so much of ourselves in trying to make a bad relationship work that we end up without enough energy to invest in meeting our own needs.

Still, breaking up might feel like a cut-off-your-nose-to-spite-your-face risk/reward choice. It's not. We deserve to have each need met in all three ways! Yet if you break up with your boyfriend because of how he treats you or because of your unfulfilled pet wants, it's perfectly natural to still feel heartbroken because you'll miss the fulfillment of the needs he did meet. That's why you'll spend part of your lovesickness scheming — making up reasons to talk to him so you can stop feeling hurt and missing him.

How can you be strong and stick to your decision? After all, we want to get over lovesickness quickly and move on so that we can be with a Prince one day. There are two ways to deal with lovesickness. One is to let yourself be self-centered and meet your own needs greedily; doing so will build your self-respect. You can discover and fulfill more needs to build your beautiful life. And don't forget: you have family and friends who can meet many of your needs and whose needs you can also meet. Even if your life is like Cinderella's — no family, no friends, not a soul in the world to meet your needs — there's still *someone* who can meet your needs: you.

To feel better when you're lovesick, do fun things that help you feel good. Focus on doing things you didn't or couldn't do while involved with Frog Guy. Do what makes you feel cared about; share your feelings with your girlfriends and let them value you. Finding other ways to meet your needs will help you disconnect from your lovesickness — from thinking and being sad, from missing the fulfillment of those needs your boyfriend did meet.

To help get through lovesickness, meet your own groups of needs — emotional, physical, intellectual and lifestyle. Here are some ways:

- Value yourself and others. Write in a journal, talk to your friends, talk to your mom, call a help line...
- Get hugs from everyone who cares about you in your life. Hug a pillow at night when you go to sleep. Hug your pet, or someone else's. Ever heard the expression "Fake it until you make it"?
- Challenge yourself to stay in the present. Don't think about seeing your boyfriend; think about *not* seeing him today. Get through each minute and each day, one at a time. Reread your Hurt List over and over. Read books.
- Use your To Do List to take special care of yourself: watch movies, listen to music, drink tea, have bubble baths, take long showers, get your hair restyled, put on nice body lotion, pick a new hobby or interest, go for a bike ride or a walk.

A second way to deal with lovesickness is to meet your needs by ignoring your beliefs, feelings and self-worth. Often, when we've been hurt so badly that we can't think clearly, we make choices to get our immediate needs met — shopping for extra goodies. You often pay for the satisfaction of these pet wants with the currency of self-respect. Fulfilling your needs in destructive ways — like going to a party, getting drunk and shagging a guy you don't even know — is both dangerous and pointless. You may be able to disconnect from your lovesickness for a moment while meeting these so-called needs, but afterward you'll feel even worse.

DO NOT do the following:

- Don't try to use your ex-boyfriend to meet your need to value or be valued. During lovesickness this becomes a super-sized need for all of us. We miss the special connection we had, so the need to value/be valued represents a desire for intimacy or closeness, and fulfillment of this need is the reward we get whenever we invest in relationships. It's also what's so hard to give up.
- Don't immediately go shopping for a new boyfriend. Take a break. Collect your lovesickness rewards: more self-knowledge and information about what you need leads to making better boyfriend choices (the learning loop). If you don't, you'll find yourself shopping at some new guy's store to feel better and to help you get through lovesickness. Easy? Yes. Fair to him? No. Helpful to you? No.
- Don't say nasty things about your ex-boyfriend (trying to get your girlfriends to hate him so that he'll become an outcast). Don't say nasty things to him, like telling him you hate him. And don't try to hurt him or make him jealous by dating his best friend.
- Do not make out or have sex with guys you don't have feelings for. You won't get your needs to be noticed or desired met this way!
- Don't avoid thinking by ignoring your brain — don't shut down. Read your Hurt List every morning if you have to!
- Don't stop working on your To Do List. Don't make poor social choices (by going to parties and getting drunk, or lying in bed all day and hiding from your life).

You made a smart choice to end a relationship with a Frog and then found the courage to do it. You respected yourself enough to refuse to settle for less than you deserve. These are huge steps forward in your life. Don't follow such a courageous and positive choice with choices that leave you feeling worse. Making a risk/reward choice just to help you through short-term pain is like taking three giant steps backward. If you're going to make bad choices after the break-up, what was the point of breaking up in the first place? Self-destructive behavior says the same thing about you that staying with a Frog does: that you don't think enough of yourself to accept what you deserve — a beautiful, Frog-free life.

don't go back!

After a break-up, any decision that makes you feel better temporarily is almost always a bad one, especially if it involves reconnecting with your ex-boyfriend. As a result of *any* break-up, you'll have moments of self-doubt and feel you made the wrong choice. You might second-guess yourself and say, "Maybe I can still grow happy with this guy without all my needs met." You miss him and it hurts, but you'll eventually reach the point where you can't even recall how sad you were about the break-up!

Until the blessed day when you no longer miss him, you and your thinking voice will probably make up reasons to call him. We all question our exit choice when we suffer from unfulfilled needs, but you must trust your own Prince/Frog List: there are *no* right reasons to call a Frog after you've dumped him. If you call your ex-boyfriend and tell him you want to work through his feelings with him, but the purpose of the call is really to work through your own feelings, you're a tricky Frogette and you're disrespecting him. If you call him to get back together with him (you've changed your mind) to make yourself feel better, only to break up again, you're a confused Frogette. If you act like Elizabeth when she made her cut-off-her-nose-to-spite-her-face risk/reward choice and broke up with Jordan on a whim, you broke up with him only because he hurt you. But now that you miss him so much you're no longer angry, you're also a confused Frogette. If you call him to say sorry for all the nasty things you said, and then get angry at him when he doesn't beg you to come back, you're a tricky Frogette.

If you do call him, he may be cold or distant, and you may be hurt all over again. He probably won't treat you the way he did before because you're not as important to him as you once were, no longer his sexy kitty. And he might wish to punish you for breaking up with him.

And if you think that going back to your Frog will cure your lovesickness, think again. First, people who care about you and listened to you talk about your hurt feelings will not relish listening this time around. The consequence: you'll feel lonely. Second, when you go back you'll still go through love-sickness; it will just be inside your relationship. And just like in Meghan's relationship with Michael, you'll reap none of the rewards of lovesickness, but you *will* experience the suffering. Worse, the lovesickness will be compounded by this conse-quence: you'll stop learning and growing. When you can't solve your Hurt List, yet you stay in a bad relationship, you turn into Michael, who could only see the world through his own needs filter. Until you leave, you'll find it hard to like yourself and it will be nearly impossible to build yourself a beautiful life.

When you don't value yourself enough to stay away from your Frog Guy, you also become the other villain in your own story. If you're still thinking you could go back to him, don't. You deserve more; any guy should be thrilled to have you in his life. You have value, but if you go back to the wrong relation-ship, you're saying, "I don't value myself. My needs don't matter." If you don't care about your needs, no one else will either. Okay, let's move on and reset your bar. Do you respect yourself enough? Ask yourself: "Do I allow a guy into my life who values me the way I value myself?" Your answer to this question should be a big fat YES. You go, girl! And by the way, it's impossible for a Frog to be the guy of your dreams anyway!

Any good relationship needs two things: trust and respect. This doesn't just mean trusting and respecting one another — it means trusting and respecting yourself. Did you trust your last boyfriend? Building a relationship with a guy means letting him close enough to share things and feelings that are important, to risk letting him hurt you. Taking this risk requires that you value yourself, that you trust and respect your boyfriend, and that he trust and respect you.

At some point in every relationship your boyfriend will hurt you. Relationship pain is a fact of life. Would you rather be hurt by a Prince — whom you trust and respect in the big picture — or by a Frog? Be careful about diving into a new relationship until you can see — and feel — that trust and respect are really there. Before you dive in, wet your toes, splash around, check how deep the water is. Make sure that when you finally do take the plunge, you'll be able to surface again.

♡ HEART-SAVING SHORTCUT: In lovesickness, do the same thing you did to manage your own feelings in the relationship: write down what you want to do in the moment (like call him) and then put your wish in the drawer. Use this tactic to work through those in-the-moment bad choices. Park that pet want!

Ask yourself this question: do you believe that your boyfriend is going to be okay? The answer should be a resounding "Yes!" You're not responsible to save your boyfriend from his bad choices. If he isn't capable of taking care of himself, you're smart to have left him. If you feel responsible for his whole life, you're wrong. You were only responsible to *add* to his happiness, not to *be* his happiness! If you're worried about him and his life, you made a good choice to exit. The break-up will be good for him too; he'll be okay (and, by the way so will you). In fact, if breaking up hurts him and he understands why, then he may learn from the experience and become more Prince-like — or at least less Frog-like — for the next girl he meets.

♡ HEART-SAVING SHORTCUT: Often when girls break up with their boyfriends and feel sad, they look back on their happy memories. Then the boyfriend calls and tries to make up. If your ex calls you to whine about how much he misses you, ask him not to. If he calls again, he's being disrespectful. If you don't stop him in his tracks, this whining might continue until you find yourself back in a bad relationship. He might sound like a new man, but don't go there! He's just a tricky or confusing Frog with great phone skills. Tell him he has to work out his feelings with someone other than you, and if he responds by telling you how important you are, rather than getting confused or upset, become the Tin Man (the guy without a heart) and hang up. Your relationship is over: you only have to fix things with yourself.

Do you know what a mantra is? It's something you repeat over and over to help you through what you need to do in your life. It can really help you stand by a tough decision you have to make, especially if you know that you might feel afraid or uncertain afterward.

When you've decided to break up, try turning your thinking voice into a mantra. Perhaps you could start with something like: "I *know* there's someone out there who's more compatible with me than you are." Then insert one of your top three Hurt List items — for example, "There's someone out there who's more compatible with me than you are. I don't feel important to you." Practice saying this over and over again to yourself *before* you break up. Afterward, this mantra will help keep you strong enough to stand by your decision. Think of the Hurt List item in your mantra as your "truth stick" and use it like a walking stick to keep yourself moving forward after breaking up. Even if your first steps are tiny and painful, they still carry you away from that relationship. Stand by your decision and before long you'll be strong enough to throw that stick away and walk confidently in any direction you choose!

growing through lovesickness

Don't ever choose to stay with a guy just because he has potential; he is who he is now, and if you can't accept him for who he is now, release him back to the pond. He isn't going to change — ever.

♡ HEART-SAVING SHORTCUT: A Frog is a guy you're going out with who *looks* like, or has the *potential* to be, a Prince but is not. You might say to yourself, "If *only* he did (or didn't) do this (or that) he'd be a Prince." But he's not going to change; if he does, the New Him won't last. So he's a Frog — for you! Wait. Guys can and do change, so can your ex-Frog become a Prince one day? Absolutely. For another girl!

There are great benefits to lovesickness. First, having experienced — probably painfully — things you didn't like in a guy, you no longer have to put up with them. Second, you learned about your unfulfilled needs by managing your Hurt List items. You now know more about your needs, and how important it is to get them met. Third, you've discovered what needs he did meet, so next time you'll know at least some of what you should be looking for. You're going to date Frogs — this fact is unavoidable but ultimately helpful. It's helpful because by going out with Frogs and experiencing both what you like and what you don't, you figure out what you need. Just don't get stuck when you discover you're with a Frog.

You've just exited from a relationship in which your Hurt List was constantly telling you that at least one of your needs was not being met. Perhaps your boyfriend was also using disrespect to get his needs met by you. Now that you're no longer with the guy, ask yourself, "Why did I stay one minute extra in a relationship with a guy when I wasn't growing happy?"

It's important to answer honestly so that you grow from your experience. If you don't, you may end up staying in a relationship with a Frog too long the next time because you're confused. If you don't take the time to figure out what needs you did or did not get met, you'll date Frogs in different packaging. Even though they might feel like different guys (and they are, of course, because they all have different traits), they'll have similar Frog warts and won't meet your needs. Many women are with Frogs simply because they haven't made the effort to learn from their Frog experiences.

♡ HEART-SAVING SHORTCUT: Know a girl who gets a new boyfriend within two weeks of dumping her last one, or being dumped by him? Usually her relationships end with a huge blowout and the discovery that the guy was not what he presented himself to be. But no matter how many relationships she goes through, she still chooses Frogs! She doesn't look at the character of each guy, so she picks the wrong guys. Over time, she gets more and more jaded about guys. Her relationships are always disastrous, but she isn't learning about herself and why she keeps making terrible choices. If she put half as much energy into knowing and loving herself as she puts into these Frogs, she'd get it.

Painful as lovesickness may be, the decision to break up with a Frog is always the right one. Taking the step to leave him deposits a huge amount of self-respect currency into your account, and using your lovesickness to gather information and to grow will help you to build better filtering skills. Lovesickness provides you with a precious opportunity to build your beautiful life, strengthen your friendship and family bonds and bring you closer to the fairy tale that is possible.

There is a Prince out there for you. To find him, recognize him and choose him, your only job is to value yourself. He'll be attracted to you because — life is a mirror! — he values himself. You'll be important to him for a great reason: because he believes that you meet all his needs within the four dating beliefs. And he'll be important to you for the same great reason. You'll experience the fairy tale that is possible.

In the next chapter you'll finally see Natalie experiencing the fairy tale that is possible for her!

NINE: *the real-life fairy tale*

Natalie has pretty much got it together. She's learned that while her kisses can't turn a Frog into a Prince, a Prince can definitely turn into a Frog. Yes, even a Prince can walk all over you to get a need met. It depends on how succulent his pet want is! In fact, anyone can croak like a Frog or waltz like a Prince — even when we have goodness running through our veins. It's called being human.

Natalie has a great bar, which she has set with the dating beliefs and self-knowledge from her own experiences, ending up with rules of conduct. For example, she changed the needs question "Can I forgive him when his actions make me really angry?" into a standard for how she lives her life: "I won't be in a relationship where I can't forgive my boyfriend's nasty or hurtful actions."

Since she now takes care of herself first, she uses her needs filter with a twist — to understand her boyfriend and others in her life. She understands her own needs and recognizes that everyone's needs are pretty much the same.

When Natalie's boyfriend gets upset, she tries to figure out which need, if any, he isn't getting met. Then she asks herself, "Is there something I can do about this?" Even if there isn't, they usually end up talking about what's wrong rather than spending their time stuck in rerun arguments. As an unmet need comes up in her relationship, she recognizes it and asks her boyfriend to meet that need. Using the skill of linking experiences with needs is how Natalie avoids life with a Frog and becomes a Prince magnet. So when she met Josh, she was finally ready to recognize, accept and build a relationship with a Prince.

natalie and josh

They met when Natalie stopped by her friend Ricky's apartment. He'd just finished redecorating and Josh had dropped in to see the results. When they were introduced she was taken with the way Josh smiled at her. She couldn't help smiling back. While she looked around the living room, she stole glances at him. He was tall and had sandy-blond hair and blue-green eyes and a body to die for — this guy was obviously an athlete. On her third stolen glance she got caught and they both smiled again, and to cover their embarrassment — he'd been sneaking glances too — they started talking about the changes to Ricky's apartment.

Natalie looked at her watch. She was late and had to run. As she was leaving, they said an awkward goodbye. She wondered if he was going to ask for her number. He didn't. Later that night she fell into bed dreaming up girly-girl strategies to run into him again. For the next few days she replayed in her mind the way she'd reacted to Josh and what they'd said. He was just so damn attractive and they'd had great banter — he'd had such excellent material.

Josh must have asked Ricky for her phone number — he calls the next day. And they step into the story of their romance. Going on dates — dancing and talking into the wee hours. Doing each other's favorite things — going to movies and hockey and basketball games, listening to music — laughing the whole time. All the while each is hungrily seeking information from the other:

NATALIE: So tell me, Josh, what do you want to be when you grow up?

JOSH: You don't think I'm grown up? I want to be a professional coach or a PE teacher.

NATALIE: I wondered if you wanted to be a pro athlete.

JOSH: I did, but I blew out my knee a few years ago. That's going to stop me from having a pro career, even if I was good enough. What about you?

NATALIE: A lawyer.

JOSH: Why a lawyer?

They also explore each other's beliefs:

NATALIE: So tell me, football guys have a nasty reputation for sharing — do you?

JOSH: Oh, you're talking about the team girls?

NATALIE: Didn't Seth and John both go out with Amy?

JOSH: Yeah. Why are you asking?

NATALIE: I'm just trying to get to know you better. I like you…I think you like me?

JOSH: Sure I do. But let's not get too serious too soon.

NATALIE: I'm just trying to figure out where your head's at.

JOSH: I've dated team girls before, but I'd never date my ex's best friend, like John's doing.

NATALIE: Last Tuesday, when you were busy — did you take another girl out?

JOSH: No, although I'm not sure at this point I wouldn't — we're kinda just friends.

NATALIE: Friends with benefits doesn't work for me. So let me know when you do know what we're doing. If you go out with another girl, tell me, okay?

JOSH: Sure. And where are you with this?

NATALIE: I'm open.

JOSH: Good answer — me too.

Natalie leaves feeling a little sad and uncomfortable. Later that night, on her way out the door to meet Josh, she puts those feelings in a drawer. The following day she meets Meghan for lunch and they catch up.

MEGHAN: Hey, you look great.

NATALIE: First you, how are you feeling? Still missing Michael?

MEGHAN: Desperately. But I'm not going back — don't worry.

NATALIE: You sure?

MEGHAN: Josh. Tell me everything.

NATALIE: He asks what I think about stuff, and he's so interesting. And it just feels so good when he holds me tight and kisses me.

MEGHAN: Hey, your favorite thing is missing — what about "He loves politics"?

NATALIE: I have you to share that with. (Laughs)

MEGHAN: (laughing) Well, I know what you share with Josh.

NATALIE: Is it that obvious?

MEGHAN: Yeah?! But have you guys figured out where you're at yet?

NATALIE: I asked him about that yesterday — he said he's not there yet...

MEGHAN: I bet he is. It's just gonna take him a little longer to figure out. Anyway, I'm so proud of you. It's good to get that question into the open. Now he knows that you expect an answer.

One night Natalie's telling Josh she has ballet tickets. She's about to ask him to go with her when he butts in.

JOSH: First I want to ask you something.
NATALIE: Okay, shoot.
JOSH: I don't want you dating other guys, okay? Let's move to the next stage.
NATALIE: Any ground rules?
JOSH: No — you?
NATALIE: Well, I know about open relationships, but I don't like sharing.
JOSH: Me neither — you're my girl.
NATALIE: Now, will you go to the ballet with me? I love it so much.
JOSH: I'd go if you were dancing, baby, but you're not.

All relationships take work — even the best ones — and one day Josh lets Natalie know that she isn't meeting his need to feel pleased.

JOSH: You're always working weekends and I have to hang alone with the guys and their girlfriends after a game. It doesn't feel right.
NATALIE: Josh, I'm paying for college.
JOSH: I know, but can't you trade off some Saturday nights?
NATALIE: I make more on Saturday nights than during the week.
JOSH: If this is going to work, you have to find a way to come sometimes.

Natalie thinks about Josh's request and respectful ultimatum and adjusts her work schedule. Now she works two

Saturday evenings a month and spends the other two with Josh and his friends — it's on their shared To Do List. The relationship is important to her, and she feels that Josh's pet want is reasonable. She sees that satisfying this want meets his need to feel important — to know that she is part of his life and makes choices that include his feelings.

Josh has a naughty habit of doing the "What about you?" Frog sidestep dance. The dance is usually performed while she's trying to discuss a serious issue with him. It isn't easy to detect, at first, as it sounds as if a discussion is going on, when it really isn't. Josh is just deflecting the heat from himself onto her:

NATALIE: Josh, you hurt my feelings when you flirted with that girl. Please don't do that anymore.

JOSH: Well, now you know how I felt when you were flirting with that guy at the Christmas dance.

NATALIE: That was months ago — we'd barely started going out. We've been going out for five months now and what you did made me really uncomfortable.

JOSH: I'm sorry — come here. Listen, you know that all I wanna do is get to know every inch of you — listen to your stories, hold your hand, kiss you.

The work of the relationship includes helping each other understand how to make their way in the world, being great sounding boards and sharing their opinions on a wide variety of issues. One day Natalie comes rushing into the café where they're meeting to grab lunch. She's in a flap.

JOSH: Hey, slow down, tell me what happened.

NATALIE: Okay, well you know my plan about becoming a crime scene investigator instead of a lawyer, right?

JOSH: Yeah.

NATALIE: Well, when I told Meghan, she went ballistic. I can't believe she wasn't supportive.
JOSH: Did you tell her why you're switching?
NATALIE: No, we didn't even get there.
JOSH: Listen, baby, she was probably just trying to make sure you made the right decision. After all, this is a big change for you. Call her later and talk about it.

Another sign that they have a mutually healthy relationship is that whenever either of them brings up an unsatisfied (reasonable) pet want, they usually get back on track with a conversation about their shared To Do List:

JOSH: Remember how we used to go out and dance all the time? How come we don't do that anymore?
NATALIE: I guess we haven't made an effort — too busy? You're always at practice and I've been swamped this term.
JOSH: I really miss dancing with you.
NATALIE: Okay, baby, let's go out Friday night and dance our butts off. You in?
JOSH: Absolutely!

No relationship, once it gets past the delicious early days, is a cakewalk. Natalie and Josh continue to challenge each other.

JOSH: Baby, I really need your help here.
NATALIE: With what?
JOSH: We have a big game on Saturday, and Coach has scheduled extra practice time every day. I have an exam and a paper due on Friday.
NATALIE: Well, I can't go to practice for you, and I can't write the exam for you...

JOSH: You could write the paper for me. You could whip it off in no time. You know how I struggle with my writing.

NATALIE: You're asking me to help you cheat on a major assignment?

JOSH: I'm gonna fail the course if I don't get this essay in. You have to help me!

NATALIE: Josh, I'm swamped now too.

JOSH: I know I should have started a long time ago, but you're so damn cute you've distracted me the whole term...

NATALIE: RIBBET! Look, you're free tonight, right?

JOSH: Yeah, after practice.

NATALIE: I'll come over at 7:30, and we can brainstorm together. I'll help you do an outline. You write a draft, and I'll look it over.

JOSH: Thanks, baby.

NATALIE: You owe me big time — next time I get tickets, you're going to the ballet.

JOSH: Anything you say, sexy teacher.

They don't bully each other into accepting beliefs, although they do challenge each other. Spotting each other's Frog words or actions has become a game for them. Whenever one of them uses a Frog action to get a need met and the other spots it, the offender is required to own up and pay a "wart fine." The fine is paid by satisfying the other person's pet wants with no negotiating — just doing.

The best part about the middle stage of their relationship is that their shields have come down as each understands more about where the other is coming from. Because Natalie's become really familiar with Josh, she knows how to please him. She's learned his favorite foods and things to do, and she understands how to meet his need to feel important, valued and accepted. She doesn't jump through hoops; she's simply thoughtful.

Each of them knows that there are two sets of needs to be understood, respected and fulfilled. Both are responsible to see that their own needs get met and to help the other meet theirs. Each considers the other's feelings and needs in their choices. For example, when Josh is in the playoffs, Natalie feels ignored. He lives and breathes the game, on and off the field. So Natalie adjusts what she expects from him (her bar), and Josh deliberately tears himself away, now and again, to satisfy her favorite pet wants. He can't satisfy them as often as he usually does, but when he sees that she's down, he's there for her. Nevertheless, they still have spats sometimes.

JOSH: Will you grab my cell from the car?
NATALIE: No way.
JOSH: Why not?
NATALIE: I'm busy. You can just as easily get it yourself.
JOSH: Somebody might score while I'm gone! Couldn't you be a sweetheart and get it for me?
NATALIE: Sure — when pigs fly!
JOSH: Aaargh.

She isn't afraid to hear what he has to say — quite the opposite — because she knows he cares for her. The last time she didn't meet a need, he made a deliberate choice not to say things he didn't mean; he didn't get frustrated or angry. Even though he wasn't happy about his unsatisfied pet want, she still felt important to him. For example, while she was on her way to that dreaded exam, he called her to wish her luck. He called again right afterward to see how it went. However, he was still pissed off, so he didn't try to please her by showing up at the door to the examination hall with a coffee, a donut and a ride to her doorstep.

Red flags show up in the middle too. Let's look at a rerun argument they've been having lately.

NATALIE: Remember when we talked about doing more things together that didn't involve your sports friends?

JOSH: I know, baby, but I've made a commitment to the team. What I do next season can't happen until next season.

NATALIE: Can't you book off to go to my cousin's wedding on the 12th?

JOSH: It's a team sport — if I'm not there we might not get into the finals.

NATALIE: What about us? I thought we were a team.

JOSH: We are, and I love being on your team.

NATALIE: You didn't make it to Meghan's birthday, to my family Thanksgiving or to my cousin's engagement party, yet we always hang out with your teammates. I want you to live in my life, too.

JOSH: I know, baby. I'm going to cut back next season. But I can't go to the wedding, so let's leave it alone now, okay?

In the middle of the relationship, you may not kiss and make up right away, as you did in the beginning, but something better happens: the person who has said no to the reasonable request is responsible to make those wonderful make-up calls. Josh is a master, and the next morning he calls:

JOSH: How are you? Have a good sleep?

NATALIE: Yes.

JOSH: Still angry at me?

NATALIE: Sort of.

JOSH: Do you still love me?

NATALIE: Yes.

JOSH: How angry are you — say, between one and ten?

NATALIE: I don't want to talk to you right now.

JOSH: Okay, but tell me you missed me last night.

NATALIE: No.

JOSH: Stop being mean to me. How come you won't say you miss me?

NATALIE: I just don't feel like it.

They hang up, both amused, but she's still a little miffed. The subsequent calls follow the same pattern, with Josh increasing the sugar dosage — usually flirting wickedly — and eventually lowering Natalie's anger reading down to zero.

what went wrong

Absolutely nothing! Natalie stepped out of the maze into the middle of a compatible relationship. She has great filtering skills, and she's set her bar — she expects to be treated the way she treats herself and others. She believes she loves herself and Josh, yet this red flag leads her to question whether she's loved in return. Red flags point to work that needs to be done in a relationship. This work is what can get you to the fairytale that is possible!

Can she find someone more compatible than Josh?" She's decided to look at the big picture of her relationship, so she fills in a Prince/Frog List for Josh.

> ♡ HEART-SAVING SHORTCUT: Only one thing stands between you and the real-life fairy tale: your bar not being set to Just Right. Once it is, ask yourself, often, whether your boyfriend measures up. This won't turn you into one of those "overanalyzing" girls — you'll simply be a girl who manages her Hurt List.

josh's prince/frog list

First, she answers the questions to fill in the Prince Section. Then she runs through the Hurt Feelings Checklist for each dating belief, making sure that any items she checks are red flags and don't include isolated incidents or unsatisfied entitled pet wants. She finds she has one unsatisfied pet want: "He doesn't make enough time for me in my life," which means she wants Josh to invest more time in their shared To Do List.

She asks herself if getting this pet want satisfied requires Josh to put her needs first, his second. Maybe it wasn't right for her to demand that he invest more time in their shared To Do List; after all, he would have to sacrifice some of his sports activities. She wants Josh to grow happy too. Is she being selfish? She's not sure.

To determine whether her need to have him spend more time with her friends and family is a genuine need or an extra goodie, she asks, "Can I give up this pet want and still respect myself?" No. She values traditions and family gatherings, and not having this pet want satisfied would stop her from growing happy. She puts this Hurt List item into the "I am the draw for him" belief in the lifestyle needs group of the Frog Section. Her rerun experiences link to her missing need to feel important to Josh.

Is Natalie being selfish? No, her bar is just right. She's simply trying to get what we all deserve: fulfillment of our genuine needs. It's okay not to like a guy's refusal to meet your needs and to try to get those needs met. If you're familiar with yourself, you'll be able to tell him why that need is important to you. And your boyfriend will have the best information you can give him to make an informed choice.

Josh is the draw for her, she likes herself and she likes him. She's just not sure that she's the draw for him. This is reflected in her Prince/Frog List. Josh gets a "Pass" in each of her emotional, physical and intellectual need groups. In the Prince Section, Natalie answered all the questions for each dating belief with a "Yes" except for "Important: Does he include my feelings and needs in his choices?" In the Frog Section, there's a match between her unmet lifestyle need and her "No" answer in the Prince Section. Perfect. No wonder, when she reaches the last row of her Prince/Frog List for her lifestyle needs group, she gets stuck between "Pass" and "Fail."

Is Josh the right guy for Natalie? Relationships don't work if living your life — meeting your own needs — hurts your boyfriend or vice versa. Finding the delicate balance of pleasing and helping each other equally in a shared To Do List can be challenging. Josh has asked Natalie to support him in his decision to meet his sports commitments. She'll have to either give up the fulfillment of this need to feel important or allow it to remain unfulfilled for a while.

Natalie knows that if the way Josh chooses to live his life really hurts her, she'll have to break up with him. Both Natalie's and Josh's feelings and needs are reasonable, and each of them is being respectful. Even if Josh chose not to quit any of his sports activities, this wouldn't be disrespectful to Natalie. His choice has to do with meeting his *own* lifestyle needs, instead of hers.

She may be stopped in her happy-girl tracks, momentarily, but she's experiencing the positive consequence of developing her filtering skills — she doesn't have a whole bunch of distractions (other unmet needs) to add to her confusion. So she uses her filtering skills to make a deliberate choice here.

In the big picture, her relationship has only one red flag, a lifestyle need: important. Her Hurt List has always been easy to manage. She trusts Josh when he says that since they've been together, meeting his own lifestyle need to be pleased has changed; he wants to make more time for their shared To Do List. For now, she believes she can accept this unmet need and still respect herself. She can wait and still grow happy until he makes himself more available. Meantime, she takes Meghan to her cousin's wedding and, though she misses Josh, has a great time.

filtering skills

The Prince Section of the Prince/Frog List will tell you if you're experiencing a compatible relationship. If you're thinking it would be hard to respond "Yes" to every need in a relationship with any guy — that your bar is set too high — think again! Try answering the Prince Section questions using your relationship with your best girlfriend — substituting hugs for affection in the physical needs group.

If we don't know what we deserve, we settle for less than we deserve. Knowing what's possible gives us something to measure our experiences against. This knowledge gives us a way to evaluate our choice and decide whether to stay or go. Your bar does what magical incidents do in fairy tales: it keeps you on track to make good choices; it helps you choose — and not choose — a boyfriend. It allows you to meet someone else's needs while maintaining your self-respect. And it gives you the confidence to give up the satisfaction of a pet want and still grow happy.

Setting your bar works for making boyfriend choices, but it also applies to other relationships in your life. Your bar indicates how you expect to be treated by co-workers, friends and family. And the Prince/Frog List can also be used as a tool to evaluate any significant relationship. You shop at your best friend's boutique and she shops at yours. She gets her needs met, too, just by meeting yours. All you have to do is adjust your bar to match the relationship's shared expectations — like Gwen did in her long-distance relationship.

natalie's dilemma

A year after Natalie and Josh start dating, she notices Anthony, who's joined her political science study group. A couple of weeks into the course, he invites her for coffee to talk about an upcoming assignment. She goes. When it's time to leave she has to tear herself away; he's incredibly interesting. That "Interesting" need grows on its own; she tries not to water the need, but it grows anyway. The next time he asks her for coffee, she doesn't go — but still the need grows, developing into a succulent pet want. She's drawn to Anthony because they share a passion for politics. She starts dressing up for study group. As the feeling becomes super-charged, she looks for a way out. What should she do? She's already chosen her Prince. She calls Meghan.

What do you do when you have a boyfriend and you find chemistry with another guy? First, look at your own life to see if you're meeting your own needs. Natalie does this, recalling that she almost made a choice about a year ago to become a crime-scene investigator instead of a lawyer. Using the learning loop (needs-choices-consequences) she decided to stay with becoming a lawyer. Now she senses that she's growing happy and everything feels just right.

Next, fill out a Prince/Frog List for your boyfriend. Did you find any unmet needs you didn't see before? (Remember the pink-top experience.) Natalie fills in a new Prince/Frog List for Josh. She answers the questions and checks off her

Hurt List items. In the dating belief "He is the draw for me," she finds a pet want that just woke up — "Interested: We run out of things to talk about all the time." She could just as easily put "We don't talk politics." In the dating belief "I am the draw for him," she finds other unmet needs: to be challenged and to see Josh come alive around her. She's confused about why these unmet needs would show up while she's with her Prince.

Early on, Meghan pointed out that "He loves politics" was missing from Natalie's ideal guy list. Yet it never got listed in Josh's Frog Section because it never made it onto her Hurt List — it cleared her bar at the time. Natalie pursued her interest in politics with Meghan, meeting her need to be challenged in this area.

Over time you'll develop a small bar for each of your needs. This little bar measures the difference between meeting needs with a silver or gold medal and/or with chemistry (a supercharge). Then again, Natalie might be having the pink-top experience. You can't miss what you don't even know exists. Sleeping pet wants can wake up inside any relationship, even a compatible one.

Natalie's in a compatible relationship. She's committed to including her boyfriend's feelings and needs in her choices. When a sleeping pet want wakes up, you have to adjust your self-knowledge — possibly reset your bar — genuine need or extra goodie? If it's a red flag, talk to your boyfriend about it. Natalie sees Josh come alive more around others than her! Maybe a year ago his own need to be pleased started to get met with only a silver medal when he withdrew from some of his sports activities. Josh is a Prince; like Natalie, he deserves to grow happy — to be with someone who wants to be with him as much as he wants to be with her.

It's hard to figure out what unmet needs you can accept and still respect yourself — to know when a pet want is a genuine need. In practice, your bar needs to be just right. Why? Being with your Prince does not necessarily mean you won't feel chemistry with another guy; in fact, it's likely that you will. What matters is that chemistry is never a substitute for self-respect or your boyfriend's Prince/Frog List. Chemistry doesn't necessarily point you to a new Prince, although it will always help you to identify unsatisfied pet wants in your relationship. However, if Natalie can't accept this unmet need in her relationship and grow happy, she'll have to exit. There can be more than one Prince in your life.

One other belief could trap you with a guy. If a sleeping pet want wakes up during your relationship with an otherwise great guy and becomes a genuine need that he can't meet, you must leave. If you believe you mustn't hurt him because he's a wonderful person who's done nothing wrong, you're mistaken. It's hard to leave someone you care about when there are no really big reasons to leave. After all, you made a commitment when you started the relationship and began to move forward. How could you break that commitment now? For the best reason of all. You guessed it: *unmet needs.*

Your own happiness is just as important as your boyfriend's. It's important to be selfish in matters of the heart. In the end, your own happiness has to come first. If it doesn't, you run the risk of turning into a person like Michael and only thinking about your own needs and nobody else's. Remember that living a beautiful life means you're able to meet your own needs and those of others. Having a relationship is a bit like flying together. Flight attendants tell you what to do if the cabin depressurizes and oxygen masks drop from the ceiling. Put your own mask on first — then help your boyfriend or grandmother. Don't help other people until you're sure you have your own oxygen supply or everyone might die — including you!

what about elizabeth?

The last time we saw Elizabeth, she was feeling that Jordan had ignored her needs last week and had begun to *just* make sexy kitty calls (at least that's how Elizabeth saw it). It turns out she expected him to be Prince-perfect. Jordan ignoring Elizabeth had more to do with him finishing up a big project at work than choosing not to meet her needs. This sounds similar too? Yes. It's just like her cut-off-her-nose-to-spite-her-face risk/reward choice, when she broke up with Jordan after he didn't call her back one night.

How did Elizabeth get past these "same-same" experiences in her relationship with Jordan? Brilliantly — by using the learning loop! She reviewed the information in the dating belief "I am the draw for him" to find a better rule for making and checking her choice in this situation. The needs question "Do I expect my boyfriend to put me above himself?" helped Elizabeth get past this situation. She adjusted her bar, resetting her expectations — to "NO".

She works at not using any little-picture experience to magically turn one of the four big-picture dating beliefs into a mistaken belief. Her reward: she doesn't turn into a drama diva as often! She makes better choices, relying in part on her past experiences and in part on her judgment as to whether a past experience (like the hasty break-up — "I'm not the draw for him") reflects the current situation ("He's ignoring me — he loves me not?"). This is how she learns and grows: she pays attention to the outcomes of her choices and she learns from them!

Paying attention helps her define what a met need is. For example, early on in her relationship with Jordan, he made all kinds of false accusations and mistook her motives for many of the things she did. Then it happened: she noticed Jordan stopped saying things like "You're only saying that to punish me" (when she wasn't); now he says "Did I hurt you? Is that why you're saying that?" (It was). And so on. And so on. These changes meant that Jordan had become more familiar with her, and perhaps even more respectful of her, and she loved this feeling. He began to see the best of who she really is and even when he wasn't sure, he gave her the benefit of the doubt — asking before judging. Using the "paying attention" skill, she'll be able to recognize what it feels like to have any one of her needs met.

After Elizabeth finished Jordan's Prince/Frog List, she sat back and took a few moments to think about what all her relationship experiences have added up to. Does she love herself? Not sure! She believes she knows and loves Jordan and feels loved in return — *for the most part*. Her Prince/Frog List confirms this!

Do Elizabeth and Jordan have work to do inside their relationship? Yes. And it's the *same* work they've been doing all along, recognizing and then telling each other when one of their needs isn't being met. And those needs discussions are *always* interesting. Sometimes Jordan or Elizabeth brings enough drama to be nominated for an Academy Award — but their needs conversations are great! Jordan has never once been cruel when he's talked to her; sure, he can talk like a Frog on occasion. ("Maybe if you paid more attention to me, I wouldn't flirt"— remember that one?) but in the big picture, he is her Prince.

Does Elizabeth know and like herself? Ensuring that her own needs get met is how Elizabeth keeps growing into the person she wants to become, in her own life and in her relationship. Experience teaches her what needs have to be fulfilled in order for her to build the life she wants — a *beautiful life*. She's closing gaps in her life between what she believes and what she does. She's watching the consequences of her choices to see whether her To Do List gets her what she needs. If it doesn't, she makes a new choice to close that gap. She's closing the gap between who she *wants to be* and who she *really is* by making deliberate choices. For example, she's chosen to work at not making those cut-off-her-nose-to-spite-her-face kinds of choices — ones she used to so easily make. She's working hard to change her ways — and it feels just right! She's also becoming less judging of others, which Jordan is happy about. And magically she is becoming less judging and more forgiving of herself. Her reward: she's living a *sweeter* kind of life. While she's not always sure what her beautiful life is, she's becoming less like the Scarecrow; she believes that she has value and she doesn't look for Jordan, Meghan or even Natalie to confirm it (at least not as much as she used to!)

Are both Natalie and Elizabeth experiencing the fairy tale that is possible? Yes. Each of their fairy tales is different, yet each is skipping along her own yellow-brick road — living a full, more respectful life, learning and growing happier and wiser with each experience. The fairy tale is a metaphor for a journey, not a destination. There is no fairy tale end state, just like there's no one great year in our life that we get to keep forever. Life always happens in ways that can bring us the unexpected — good, bad and everything in between. Life is a journey. Applying self-respect in your life, making deliberate choices and using the learning loop allow you to wake up growing happy and with enough energy to get through any struggles that come along. It also helps you see and appreciate when you've got it right — when you are truly growing happy — and to know that you really deserve it!

Who knows, Natalie may dump Josh, go out with Anthony and find herself lost in love and life — it's possible. But it doesn't matter! Life can throw whatever at either Elizabeth or Natalie — both are equipped with *more* self-knowledge, information and tools than before to not only choose and build a relationship with a Prince but also recognize and dump a Frog (sooner rather than later). Besides, everyone goes through times in their life when they need extra help; we've all been there and done that — and even with our feet planted on the yellow-brick road, we'll need that help again!

Is there a difference between Elizabeth's and Natalie's fairy tales? Yes! Both Elizabeth's and Natalie's unique pet wants link to two different sets of needs in two *very* different relationships. Yet they both get the same yummy reward: the consequence of understanding yourself and your needs: getting better at picking a guy who'll help meet them. For example, Elizabeth, who is a songwriter, is constantly challenged with creative problem-solving. And she loves how Jordan doesn't challenge her with heavy-duty intellectual stuff over coffee. In contrast, Natalie now knows she needs to be challenged by her guy over coffee concerning what's happening in local politics.

One last Frog trap. As long as we know a guy is a Frog (for us) if he fails any of our four needs groups — emotional, physical, intellectual and lifestyle — we can avoid this trap. Remember: in the Prince/Frog List a guy either passes or fails in each one of our groups of needs. Naturally, there will be occasions when our guy doesn't just get a pass but merits an A+. Say in every conversation, like Natalie, you feel "awakened," earning your guy an A+ standing in your intellectual needs group. In the big picture when a guy gets an A+ in one needs group, we'll find it hard to call him a Frog even when he's failed, or could fail, all three of our other needs groups! Beware: a Frog might seem to be a Prince when he does a good job of filling up only one of your needs groups (your physical needs come to mind here), while he leaves all the others stark empty.

♡ HEART-SAVING SHORTCUT: Any guy who meets your needs within each of the four dating beliefs is a Prince. He doesn't have to be a star in any one needs group; he just needs a pass. This knowledge will help you to avoid a boyfriend who satisfies only your wants, and let you build a life with *the* guy who meets your genuine needs.

last words

You now have great filtering skills and excellent tools — a Hurt List and a Prince/Frog List — to figure out if your boyfriend is the right guy for you. Setting your bar with the dating beliefs is how you get great filtering skills, and working with the learning loop is how you get the information you need to answer the big-picture question: "Can I find someone more compatible than my boyfriend?" If you can, your boyfriend is a Frog. If you have a great bar and you can't, he's a Prince.

If your bar isn't set properly, you might find yourself accepting your boyfriend's warts and life-with-a-Frog experiences (holding on to your mistaken beliefs). How high your bar is determines what kinds of behavior you accept and don't accept from a boyfriend (or anyone else for that matter), and what you accept is directly connected to your own sense of value. Do you ever find yourself thinking something like: "I love my boyfriend; he's very loving, but he has a bad temper and he thinks I'm always cheating"? If so, your bar is still too low. Take a deep breath, then kick that Frog back to the pond. Tell him: "I deserve an extraordinary man. No one treats me the way you did and gets to have me in his life." Now reset your bar.

♡ HEART-SAVING SHORTCUT: Do not think that making a list of your boyfriend's good points (pros) and bad points (cons) can replace a Prince/Frog List. Why not? Because a Prince/Frog List helps you to deliberately match your needs to your experiences, which is how you learn and grow. It's how you come to know how you deserve to be treated. And how you click your own heels together three times and wake up! If you use a pros-and-cons list, then at the very least throw the pros out the window and deal with what really matters, which is whether you can accept all of the cons and still respect yourself.

Until you value yourself, you'll probably be afraid to go out with a Prince. Subconsciously you understand that life is a mirror: if you don't feel good about yourself — if you don't like yourself — you'll make choices that reflect that lack of self-worth. You'll see a Frogette in your reflection if you're insecure, and a Princess if you know you deserve a Prince.

A relationship must reinforce self-respect and value — yours and his. Self-respect is the primary source for building that supportive little voice inside you, your thinking voice, the one that's full of confidence and says, "You go, girl!" It's the little voice that tells you when you can give up that pet want and still be happy. It's the little voice that cheers you on and tells you, "Yes, you should ask him to stop doing that" or "Yes, ask him to do more of this." It's the little voice that tells you not to listen to nasty people. This voice affects how we interact in all of our relationships — it's *the voice of our value*.

What does the voice of your value sound like? Is it full of certainty or self-doubt? Praise or criticism? You'll know you respect yourself when you hear a kind, truthful and skeptical voice, when you're no longer afraid to see your own truth or listen to someone else's. Your "thinking voice" will become quiet, even when you listen to someone tell you respectfully what they don't like about you. You'll finally take that magical leap — you'll truly value yourself, and — Poof! — you'll become a woman who works hard and gets what she really needs (and deserves) in her life.

When you've recognized your value, you'll be in a beautiful life where you can choose your Prince and live happily ever after with him. He'll be the right person for you, and you for him. You'll joyfully meet each other's needs just to add to each other's happiness, without giving up the needs you're respon-sible to meet yourself. This is true compatibility. Because you respect and value yourself, you'll know in your heart that you deserve to be respected and valued. You'll also respect and value your Prince — and others around you — *as much as they respect and value you!* Life is a mirror. This is the fairy tale that is possible.

A wise woman once told her daughter: "You choose your life by the partner you choose." If you choose a man you can learn and grow with, your love will be genuine and strong. By opening ourselves up to another person, we eventually see and accept ourselves through his eyes, too — from the outside in. So the longer love lasts, the more completely we know and love ourselves. And the more we know and love ourselves, the more we can love others and life itself. You'll be able to get through the struggles in life and contribute to the world beyond you. You'll grow into one of those beautiful women with sparkling eyes. Even when you're old, you'll be beautiful.

So how will you know when you've built yourself a beautiful life? How does it feel when your needs get met? How does it feel when you respect yourself? How does it feel when the people in your life respect you? How does it feel to be able to do the right thing because you know better? How does it feel to approach your difficulties (even big ones) knowing you'll overcome them no matter what? How does it feel when the wonderful things in life just seem to flow to you? When you know what all of these things feel like, you'll know you've built yourself a beautiful life.

Choose a Prince — a guy who fits you like Cinderella's slipper fit her. Believe in yourself. Go build your own happy ending. You have the skills for living a beautiful life — to keep yourself safe from harm and free from pain, and to become the loved and loving person you want to be. Godspeed!

acknowledgements

Writing Frog or Prince? has been an extraordinary journey, and I owe sincere thanks to many people. I have been one very lucky woman. This book would not be what it is if I hadn't had some superheroes in my back pocket. Here they are: Dr. Brian Harris and Arnold Smith, to whom I turned to when I found myself in need of clarity and knowledge; Ross Lonergan, who lovingly edited every sentence to make the book clear and succinct; and my own Prince—thank you for everything, especially for taking the journey with me to build our own happy ending.

A big fat thank you to my family—to my niece Kaiya, who at the age of six taught me why Cinderella respected herself. To my son for his love and invaluable feedback. To my Mom, who goes above and beyond that moniker every day. Ditto for my sister. And my brother. And a special thanks to my sister in-law. Additionally I'd like to thank Juliana Gillespie and Candace Waldron for their valuable input in the early days, and Maggie, for the bed-making scene.

I would also like to thank the following readers, who gave their time, encouragement and criticism: Kathy Audia, Tavia Audia, Teresa Bajan, Anne Bougie, Johanna M. Bates, Patrick

Bonkemeyer, Stephanie Bonkemeyer, Eunice dela Cruz, Tatiana Chinkis, Judy Gravino, Kristan Moran, Sharan Doman, Sherry Doman, Ricky Doman, Darcia Doman, Kim Ferguson, Neil Gillanders, Maki Hanawa, Meho Karalic, Wendy Lukasiewicz, Jill Masters, Patty Milsom, Maggie Milsom, Deljeet Parmar, Michelle Phillips, Martin Renaud, Laird Rice, Dianne Taylor, Tralene Van Laethem and Dr. Liz Zubeck.

about the author

Kaycee Jane, 46, has a degree in business adminis-tration and extensive experience in the corporate world. She lives in Vancouver, British Columbia, where she's com-pleting an Executive MBA at Simon Fraser University. She has two children, a son and a daughter.

ISBN 1425169384

9 781425 169381